58

1.00

FOLK SCULPTURE USA

FOLK SCULPTURE USA

edited by Herbert W. Hemphill, Jr.

The Brooklyn Museum

Los Angeles County Museum of Art

Published for the exhibition
Folk Sculpture USA
The Brooklyn Museum, March 6 - May 31, 1976
Los Angeles County Museum of Art, July 4 - August 29, 1976

*This exhibition was organized with the aid of
a grant from the National Endowment for the Arts
in Washington, D.C., a Federal agency.*

Front cover: The Bicycle Boy trade sign was made by the
owner of a bicycle shop in the Greenpoint section of
Brooklyn, New York, *circa* 1922. Painted wood and metal,
height 40″. *The Brooklyn Museum.*

Back cover: Miss Liberty, probably Connecticut, *circa* 1910.
Painted wood and sheet metal, height 82″. *Collection of
Michael and Julie Hall.*

Frontispiece: Dated 1889 by the newspaper in his hand,
the Newsboy hung on the *Pawtucket Record* building,
Rhode Island. The similarity between this trade sign and
the well-known Colonel Sellers at Cooperstown, New York,
suggests a possible common origin. Painted wood,
height 42″. *Collection of Michael and Julie Hall.*
(Photograph by Thomas B. Wedell.)

Designed and published by The Brooklyn Museum,
Division of Publications and Marketing Services,
188 Eastern Parkway, Brooklyn, New York 11238.
Type set by Foto-Spectrum Inc., Connecticut
Printed in the USA by CLR Inc., New York.

ISBN 0-87273-055-7
Library of Congress Catalog Card Number 75-37338

Available to the Trade only through
Universe Books, 381 Park Avenue South,
New York, NY 10016.

Foreword

by Michael Botwinick
Director
The Brooklyn Museum

Folk art—the bright colors, the unpolished look, the vigor, the directness—images we have been building of these complex expressions of folk traditions for some forty-five years have reached a new peak of popularity and serious attention. In separating folk sculpture from the context of folk art, certain suggestive ideas have begun to emerge. One begins to suspect that attitudes about folk art have been more revealing about the beholder than the maker. At times, folk art may be taken as a tonic against the slickness of other art forms, or conversely, its separateness and naiveté may be taken as a reaffirmation of the viewer's sophistication. But no matter. Every style, every art movement, goes through a series of fragmented perceptions while its outlines strengthen and make themselves clear. Given the clearer focus of concentration on one form—sculpture—we sense that we are on the verge of some new steps in our comprehension of this art form.

In organizing this exhibition we have produced the "undefinitive" show—the exhibition that raises more questions than it answers. In the provocative essays that follow, no capsule history is proposed, no attempt is made to finally define the aesthetics, no comprehensive iconography, ontology, or cosmography is considered. And no attempt has been made to impose a consistent viewpoint or a single conclusion. More than anything, we are pushing through to a new understanding of folk sculpture. No universal system of classification of folk sculpture has been established. The differing perspectives that each of this catalogue's contributors brings to the problem add to each other. If you approach them as a series of tools that can provide a deeper and richer understanding of what you see, then you will be in tune with the spirit of our approach to the exhibition. It is only if you look to one idea or another as a definitive approach to folk sculpture that the differences seem irreconcilable. And a definitive approach has not been our intent.

We hope *Folk Sculpture USA* will provide basic groundwork. We hope we have offered a series of insightful perspectives that turn the problem, first a few degrees this way, then a few degrees that way. We hope that we have asked some questions that will occupy scholars, collectors, artists, museum and gallery visitors, and many others for some time to come. We hope that we have pushed forward the realization that, when used in the context of folk sculpture, the word "simple" is a descriptive term relating to certain questions of style and not a guide to our perception of the whole.

We have deliberately let the disagreements, the decidedly different avenues of pursuit, remain. But there is a sure medicine for the consternation that will inevitably accompany the enlightenment the discussions provide. Step over them for a moment and go right to the objects. They have it all. They have the force, the self-assurance, the conviction that they are meaningful objects that will challenge you. It is not surprising that, as in all exhibitions, *Folk Sculpture USA* starts and ends with the object. Everything else is just a matter of our trying to catch up.

Breaking ground in a new area is always a difficult business. This exhibition acd catalogue would not have been possible without the efforts of many people. For all of those who assisted on this project, we express our thanks. Our special gratitude is due to Herbert W. Hemphill, Jr., who has guided so much of this project. Thanks also go to Robert Bishop, the author of *American Folk Sculpture*, who opened all his research files to us; to Julie and Michael Hall, whose knowledge of the field and their special vision provided an additional degree of discernment; to Jim Kronen, whose ideas helped spark the exhibition; to Cyril Nelson, the editor of several books in this field, who gave freely of his materials; and to Julia Weissman, whose support helped immeasurably. Particular gratitude goes to Lynn Kohl, for adding another dimension to the exhibition, and to Michael Kan, for his tremendous effort in spite of the press of many other responsibilities. And finally, the appreciation of everyone involved with *Folk Sculpture USA* goes to Sarah Faunce, for her professionalism, gentle good humor, patience, and commitment. She rescued us all many times.

It is assumed that these Hessian soldiers of the early 19th century made up one whirligig, since they have only been separated recently. Painted wood, height of tallest figure 27". *Mr. and Mrs. Harvey Kahn* and *Mr. and Mrs. Robert Peak.*

Introduction

by Herbert W. Hemphill, Jr.

Ever since the public became aware of American folk art and accepted it as a legitimate art form, it has been treated largely as a quaint reminder of the nation's manners and mores. The functional or purely decorative aspects of the work were stressed, and folk art was almost always presented with an underlying assumption that its production was a thing of the past. The premises on which *Folk Sculpture USA* were organized differ from these views.

An attempt has been made to survey two hundred years of three-dimensional folk art with no reference to the functional or decorative appeal of individual pieces. Each work was chosen for its qualities as a work of art and selection was based solely on aesthetic grounds. Craft guild type products such as figureheads, show figures, and carousel carvings are not included. Despite their obvious merit, these objects, produced in shops by trained carvers and their apprentices, do not reflect the vision of an individual artist. Company weather vanes that were produced in factories from molds, with only the details supplied by individual craftsmen, were also excluded.

It is commonly believed that the production of folk art ended with the Industrial Revolution. But folk sculpture is, if anything, produced in greater abundance today than ever before. What has been called the flowering of American folk art (1776–1876) will, in retrospect, come to be seen as merely its budding. *Folk Sculpture USA* includes a fair number of works from the twentieth century; all are powerful refutations of the notion that folk art is, by definition, antique. An important and exciting outgrowth of the breadth of this survey is the realization that a piece from the early 1800's and one from 1910 (the *Hession Soldier Whirligig* and *Miss Liberty*) have a genuine formal relationship—surely an indication that a viable tradition is at work.

The pieces in *Folk Sculpture USA* are powerful, visceral expressions, drawing their strength from an amalgam of indigenous traditions and the personal vision of the artists—visions which seem almost obsessive at times. This obsessive quality is generally ignored in surveys of American folk art. Folk art is appreciated because it is pretty, or quaint, or because it fits into some sort of imaginary, idealized decor or life style. One explanation for the predilection for the pretty rather than the powerful lies in the continuing influence of *The*

7

Index of American Design. The *Index*, sponsored by the federal government to record the handicrafts of preindustrial America, is a monumental compilation of drawings, photographs, and some actual materials featuring the decorative arts. Published in 1950, it continues to have an enormous influence on the field. The purpose was worthy, but because the *Index* was an attempt to record *all* the extant good material, it is sometimes confusing and harmful. It conditions the choices made by the pedantically oriented.

The attempt here is to emphasize primarily those pieces that would not appear in the *Index* and that have been ignored or misinterpreted for so long. Certainly the *Indian Squaw and Scout*, made early in the nineteenth century, represents fairly well known figure types. But the treatment is far removed from the standard cigar store Indians. The *White Head* is probably from a ball-toss game in a carnival or amusement park. As such, it can be seen as an interesting artifact from turn-of-the-century America. But if one regards it as a work of art, one is struck by its strange, almost surreal quality. *Black Slave*, found in New Orleans, was probably a trade sign for a slave auction and is an important object in the narrative of the social history of the United States. But it is also a figure of almost frightening intensity. That intensity, no doubt, had something to do with the private obsessions of the artist.

The reclusiveness of much of folk art is one of its primary characteristics. Certainly no artist works in complete isolation; the aesthetics of any culture permeate all levels of society. But the works in *Folk Sculpture USA* are produced, by and large, by individuals or groups that are outside the mainstream of American life, outsiders who are free from the dogmas and restrictions that the dominant culture (and its academic art world) imposes. The harsh, linear quality of *Miss Liberty* owes little to the classical tradition that inspired craft guild type figureheads. Just as *Black Slave* is an expression of a single artist's obsession, the *Death Cart* from the Penitente sect in New Mexico was made within an insular subculture and is an expression of the entire sect's obsessions.

The *White Head* and the *Death Cart* are pieces of great power. They aren't pretty and they aren't quaint. Yet, because of their sheer strength, they are effective works of sculpture. In them we see the constant regeneration and rejuvenation of a primal creative spirit, an urge, as basic as the life force, to reproduce the image of life. *Folk Sculpture USA* is a selection of vigorous objects made by untrained American artists over the last two hundred years.

Folk Sculpture USA and its catalogue are both the result of a community effort. I would like to express my heartfelt thanks to the Director and staff of The Brooklyn Museum. Their professionalism and enthusiasm made so much possible.

White Head, *circa* 1900. Painted wood, height 13¼".
The Margaret Woodbury Strong Museum.

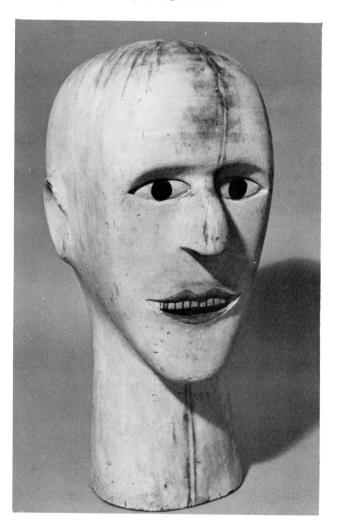

8

Authority figures are common subjects for whirligigs. They stand, pompously bearing all the accoutrements of their power. Then the wind comes up and they begin to whirl and flail about, looking silly and deflated.

Left: Railroad Conductor Whirligig, *circa* 1900. Painted wood, height 15¼". *Private Collection.*

Below: Policeman Whirligig, *circa* 1870. Painted wood, height 8¾". *Private Collection.*

Folk Sculpture without Folk

by Daniel Robbins
Visiting Professor, History of Art
Dartmouth College

Left: Despite the natural grace and suitability of the form, the swimmer is an extremely rare subject for a weather vane. New Hampshire, 1870's. Painted wood, length 38". *The Marvill Collection.*

Below: Nude Female Figure, New Hampshire, 1880's. Wood, height 6". *The Marvill Collection.*

One of the most influential but muddled aspects of American art history emerged around 1930 with the general acceptance of folk art as art. During the twenties, occasional museum exhibitions had explored this new realm with growing confidence in its validity. But the most telling signal of folk art's arrival in the art public's consciousness was the opening, in September 1931, of the American Folk Art Gallery, established under the wing of The Downtown Gallery. The establishment of "a kind of laboratory devoted altogether to American folk expression in the Fine Arts"[1] indicated the existence of a market, the most certain sign that a taste initially fostered by artists and their friends had been accepted by a wider circle.

One explanation for the rise in awareness of folk art lies in the sentiment, growing throughout the twenties, that the naive, the peasant, the savage, unspoiled by the corrupting factors of modern civilization—especially factory standardization and depersonalization—natural-ly produced work of innate value. When The Brooklyn Museum presented an early exhibition of Congo art in April 1923, the *New York Times* critic wrote of the magnetic appeal of this little known art "to a small group of enthusiasts" who saw in it the source of a new progressive movement in the art of the white man. "Their reason for thinking it progressive is, to speak quite seriously, their knowledge of the limitations of the Negro mind, of the fact that the Negro mind beyond a certain point rejects instruction, is inaccessible to scholarship, remains primitive and therefore keeps basic ideas which are not frittered away by the invasion of the supplementary, superficial and extraneous."[2] (The contemptible, racist assumptions about blacks in this review have been discarded. Is there any reason to assume that they should be more applicable to other Folk?) Straightforward expression, instinctively attained, undestroyed by civilization's complexity was the order of the time, either for those who thought it beautiful or those who found it repellent. In either case, elemental expression was at its heart. Advocates thought this force would rejuvenate our own art while scoffers found such unadulterated concentration of feeling abhorrent precisely because it lacked refinement, a quality they regarded as fundamental to fine art.

During the last half century it has become increasingly commonplace to view the recognition of America's

11

Unlike other decoys, which were used to attract their own kind, owl decoys were used to lure flocks of crows so that they could be shot. Since this was a less common way of protecting cornfields than using scarecrows, owl decoys are quite rare. New Jersey, early 20th century. Painted wood with glass eyes and leather ears, height 14¼″. *Herbert W. Hemphill, Jr.*

folk heritage as a consequence of the alteration of aesthetic values caused—indeed imposed—by the gradual acceptance of modern art. The discovery of African and Oceanic art by Picasso and Matisse was followed a little later by the discovery of American folk painting and sculpture by Robert Laurent and Elie Nadelman. For a time these several modes of art (primitive, folk, modern) appeared to be related in a fundamental way.

Beyond the admiration of modern artists, there were a number of reasons why the works of artists such as Rousseau, the art of primitive people, and American folk art were all identified as crucially important in the early thirties. The imagined community among all primitive art—a community that extended to include the work of children, lunatics, and subconscious man, as well as the work of people from the most diverse cultures in distant times and once remote places—was born, in part, as a reaction to the virulent controversy excited by modern art. Detractors of modern art asserted that it was NOT art; that all modern tendencies were equally degenerate; that direct and simple feeling was inappropriate to the accumulated culture and refinement of centuries of tradition.[3] The defense against these coarse charges slipped into an easy admiration for the honesty, sincerity, and universal expressiveness of all that was attacked. The appeal of such simplicity was understandably great, especially at a time when high art in modern sculpture was dominated by the idea that force and communication of individual personality could be achieved through "direct" attack. Works were sanctified that seemed to hark back to periods when vision was fresh or to stages in life when conventions had not yet corroded personal spontaneity. Vigor and raw strength came to be identified with meaningful invention and the two were frequently confused.

It can be said with sympathy and certainty that, around 1930, unfamiliarity and even hostility to the new artistic values led both defenders and apologists to blur important and crucial distinctions. Robert Goldwater's *Primitivism in Modern Art*, written in 1936 and first published in 1938 under the title *Primitivism in Modern Painting*, brought intellectual order into an area that previously could only be described as chaotic. Prior to its publication, writers on art made positive identifications among primitive art of all types and between the striving of modern artists and primitive art. This confusion was most often manifested in the gross equation of honesty or sincerity of expression with the unfamiliar forms possessed of such direct force. Goldwater's study cut across the blur by carving out the intellectual and historical categories that describe distinct arts produced in different contexts and by situating the growth

Above: This pair of heron decoys, like the owl on the opposite page, are examples of functional objects that, to the modern eye, achieve a satisfying simplicity of sculptural form. The herons (*circa* 1870) were probably made either on Long Island or in New Jersey. Wood, length 43½″ and 37″. *Memorial Art Gallery of the University of Rochester.*

Right: Horse with Fringe, found in Indiana, *circa* 1870–80. Stained wood with silk fringe and metal shoes, height 20½″. *Raymond Saroff.*

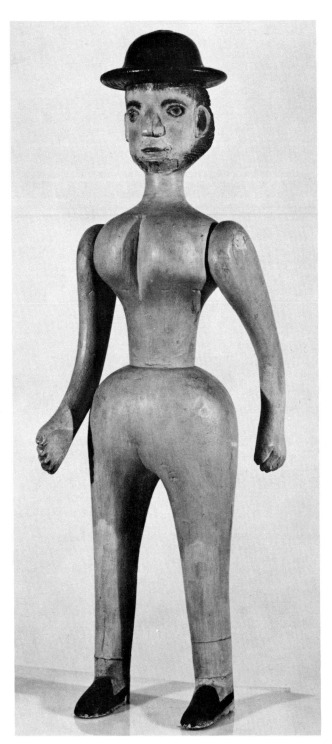

Above: The shape of this figure's beard and hat are characteristically Amish. The figure undoubtedly wore actual clothing originally and may have been a doll. Pennsylvania or Ohio, early 20th century. Wood, height 28″. *Mr. and Mrs. Leo Rabkin.*
Far right: Bull's Head, found in South Dakota, *circa* 1950. Painted wood, height 19″. *Roger Brown.*

of the whole concept of primitivism within modern Western art history.[4]

Since 1938 serious historical study has discovered a set of traditions and concerns out of which the artist created for a community for almost every category of art once lumped together as primitive; only in the realm of folk art has research not yet yielded a similar pattern. It seems that the level of our understanding of American folk art, particularly sculpture, has remained very much as it was when it first achieved popularity. Judging from some recent publications,[5] even the tenor of current appreciation of American folk sculpture is couched in a language astonishingly similar to that of forty or fifty years ago.

This language and the concepts that form the structure of its grammar are based on an erroneous identification of the aesthetic values and the appearance of certain works by modern artists with those of folk artists. It fails to take into account the complexities inherent in the production of each kind of art and is especially neglectful of the careful study of folk art. This attitude is summarized in the constantly repeated litany that the art produced by "truly American folk: everyday people out of ordinary life, city and suburban and small town and country folk" is "unaffected by the mainstream of professional art—its trained artists, trends, intentions, theories, and developments."[6]

What is it that has so curiously retarded the study, although not the appreciation, of American folk art? Even the study of folk crafts has advanced far beyond the level where it is considered the result of the untutored or purely instinctual expression of simple and naive people. Studies such as those of John T. Kirk[7] demonstrate the relationship between high style and country furniture, and research has advanced the precision with which we can date a piece and our ability to pinpoint its regional origin, not only by reference to the sources of its forms in Europe (where the same process also has been a matter of careful study recently).

Why, then, is folk art relatively untouched by both traditional and new scholarship?[8] There are at least two reasons, each complex, and both related to the larger question of the definition of current and past art. The first is the continued attractiveness of the democratic notion that simple and untutored Folk can create work that rivals in value the selfconscious production of highly trained and sophisticated artists. The second is the still growing power of the idea that interested society can stamp its own artistic values upon almost any kind of object, that each man who approaches life as an artist will find art and will find it to the extent that he himself is creative. This is an extension, and perhaps

Left: Edgar Alexander McKillop (1878–1950) was a blacksmith and inventor in Balfour, North Carolina, who admired his contemporary and fellow-inventor, Henry Ford. When Greenfield Village was established in 1929, he gave the new museum the figure of a boy with an eagle. *Circa* 1929. Walnut, height 51½″. *Greenfield Village and Henry Ford Museum.*

Far right: Centaur, Utica, New York, mid-19th century. Mr. Dines. Painted wood, height 22½″. *Private Collection.*

a particularly American extension, of a special contribution to modernism that is focused in the work and attitude of Marcel Duchamp: the found object.

The democratic attitude that crystallized so long ago and fused all forms of primitive art into one unsophisticated but expressive lump made connections between all forms of the art of primitive people and those of American folk art. It justified these relationships in the modern artist's admiration for Henri Rousseau, the modern primitive, the first and still quintessential example of the quality and intensity of an artist who was presumed to have developed entirely outside the conventions of what was then considered high art.

A brief discussion of Rousseau's place in the rise of primitivism gives some indication of the errors to which folk art enthusiasts have long been prone. In 1935 Goldwater wrote that "the enthusiasm for the work of Henri Rousseau and the other misnamed Sunday painters was based on the naive quality found or imagined in these productions. But these realists of the imagination were far from creating instinctively." Rather, they were creating "out of a tradition and for a community."[9] In *Primitivism in Modern Art*, he wrote that "true Folk art is almost always anonymous, at least it is always part of, understood by and reabsorbed into the environment that produced it."[10] Do Rousseau and his work fit these criteria?[11]

Rousseau's work was the result of his intentions rather than a "collective conscience." By dint of perseverance, unremitting work, and a sense of art's importance, Rousseau "perfected a means which we take to have completely suited his purpose." But had he more means, he would have served his purpose better, and the consonance between the technique and the ideals that pleased the modern viewer might not have been so satisfactory had Rousseau really been able to paint like Bouguereau. For the early admirers of Rousseau, there was a subtle irony in the disparity between his imperfect means and the high art ends he had in mind. The sophisticated public enjoyed seeing the high ends unconsciously satirized by the slight jolt between the almost polished technique and the ideals, enjoyed the idea that the high ideals were uncritically accepted, with the corresponding implication that such ideals—those of Bouguereau—could only be accepted by the naive.

Of course, beyond the readily intelligible high art intentions, the details of Rousseau's iconography and symbolism were personal, "deriving from experiences apart from a close familiarity or knowledge of the conventions of the ideology he wished to express." Rousseau is a genuinely interesting artist within strict limitations because, although his ambitions were high, the content

17

Nineteenth-century folk sculpture of metal is usually in the form of a flat silhouette or molded three-dimensional shape. The Standing Cockerel is rare in its use of cut metal sheets to construct a three-dimensional form, reminding us of the discoveries of early 20th-century constructivism. Connecticut. Painted metal, height 24⅝". *From the Smithsonian Institution, National Museum of History and Technology, Eleanor and Mabel Van Alstyne American Folk Art Collection.*

Great Northern Loon Decoy, Penobscot Bay, Maine. Painted wood, length 26". *Private Collection.*

Peacock, New Hampshire, 1840's. Painted wood, length 27". *The Marvill Collection.*

of his art is considerably less high than he thought. It stands in relation to academic idealism in the same ratio as his technique does toward the canons of academic realism in which he believed. We encounter here another constant and deeply moving characteristic of the naive artist: Rousseau's belief in the importance of painting in his own life, his "unselfconscious acceptance" of the value of art in the life of the community. This is the only unselfconscious aspect of Rousseau's work. Everything else—the ideals and the means—was derived from the conventions of high art.

Furthermore, Rousseau's community was that of European civilization, not the isolated and special sensibilities of the men and women who lived in his *quartier*. There is no reference to any special set of social or intellectual values that embody such things as the difficulties of material life, coarse or sordid surroundings, or toil. One cannot (although many tried in the twenties and thirties)[12] make of Rousseau an artist whose work was part of, understood by, and reabsorbed by the environment that produced him. His work can only be understood and appreciated in its double relationship to the high art of his time that he himself took as example and those artists who, departing from it, chose him as a kind of mascot.

Since the thirties, Rousseau's art has been subject to the same methods of scrutiny developed and once reserved for the more conventional symbols of individual genius in Western culture. His compositions and themes have been analyzed and traced to their sources.[13] His continued importance for purposes of discussing the larger question of folk art is the astonishing persistence of the notion that he (or Clarence Schmidt or Simon Rodia or Edgar Tolson) was the living synthesis of an anonymous multitude of humble artisans, from sign and house painters to the decorators of traveling shows; that he (and they) represents the vision of the common people; that through him, mysteriously without the intervention of guides from the instructed classes, the common people have found plastic and permanent form.[14]

A far more sophisticated and enduring approach to the accommodation of primitivism (including folk art) to civilized modern taste was put forward by James Johnson Sweeney in his exhibition "Modern Primitives" at the Renaissance Society at the University of Chicago in the summer of 1931. Sweeney maintained that the community of the primitive is to be found in the "plastic relations of the design, with a subordination of the technical and naturalistic representational elements to them." The universality of plastic elements, Sweeney noted, is not—as popularly conceived—attributable to "untutored technique or even naïveté of viewpoint." It is in plastic relationships among elements of design that one finds the chief characteristic of those works that mark the first flourishing of all great art traditions and go by the name of primitive. In Sweeney's view, which recognized the operation of tradition, the "expressive" element was relegated to a secondary role, and attention was focused almost exclusively on the plastic or structural elements in design, often yielding concise descriptions of decorative motifs, carefully trying to distinguish decoration and plasticity from mere patternism.[15]

Following the Sweeney approach of the community of plastic relations, American folk art provided a tempting basis for demonstrating that the unschooled masses had an innate understanding of plastic or formal relationships and therefore might respond favorably to abstract art. Less vigorous, but more pervasive, was the view that contemporary production would be swept forward by the discovery of a tradition that demonstrated that art belonged to all the people.[16]

One of the most interesting aspects of the acceptance of modern art in the United States is the very special place within it that was assumed by American folk art. This has to do with the internal collapse of what had, up until the arrival of modern art, been regarded as high art. In view of this sudden foundering of values, a need developed to discover a tradition out of which one might explain the emergent triumphs of a *new* high art: modernism. This was the role thrust upon folk art. It furnished, almost overnight, an unbroken American tradition with a clear relationship to what was being done by leading American artists in the early thirties. The idea that folk art constituted a two-hundred-year-old unbroken tradition of all that was characteristically American appeared highly attractive. It provided a background "solidifying and enriching a nation's fund of tradition" and established "the sense of continuity so vital to the health of contemporary art in any era."[17]

The importance of this issue—the existence or definition of an American art—is underscored by the November 1931 *Creative Art*, which was entirely devoted to the new American Renaissance. Ten authorities discussed whether there was such a thing as American art, whether American painting and sculpture revealed a "native stamp."[18] These discussions reached no absolute consensus, but for those who sought a positive answer, folk art provided eloquent proof of a native tradition. Thus, at a time when abstract art was already being attacked from certain quarters as yet another decadent product of European civilization, the intertwining ingredients that exalted primitive folk expression were used as much to provide a basis for the new native regionalist school, developing in the wake of

19

a revived distrust of internationalism, as for the universal community of people's expression based on purely plastic elements.

The upheaval caused by the penetration of modern art into the consciousness and lives of civilized Americans gradually caused another, also very young, "native" tradition to be widely regarded as a false start. Hudson River landscapes were put into attics, marble sculpture was hauled into cellars or junked. Museums traded Innesses for masters of popular realism. Nowhere was this abandonment of the older tradition more evident than in the eclipse of high sculpture in the Beaux Arts tradition. One of the most telling consequences of the removal of these objects from public consideration was its effect on the study of folk art. Placing the Beaux Arts tradition to one side removed the possibility of comparison, and folk art remained isolated from the high art traditions the abandoned forms represented.

Folk art had indeed triumphed. It was collected; it had a market; it even provided a tradition for contending traditions; it was a source for whatever wanted proof on the contemporary scene. Advocates of universal abstraction and advocates of native expression drew equal inspiration and almost *ex cathedra* authority from its forms.

This balance, however, was brief. As modernism lengthened its own tradition, folk art was often seized upon by those who looked back toward a time of imagined simplicity, when every man was an artist and art was clearly relatable to a craftsman-like impulse that people appreciated because they understood its requirements. Thus we find in the current revival of the idea of folk art, especially in the distinction made between folk art and folk craft,[19] the arguments of the thirties being repeated. There is an assumption that, because folk art remains connected to the "organic nature of things," it is sensuous, vitalistic, and the opposite of abstract art. The folk artist is made, once again, to report the state of nature in the absence of intellectualism; he is denied that fundamental link with society's continually evolving ideal of art. Like a serf to his land, the folk artist remains chained to the organic nature of things—as if there were an organic nature of things!

The fact that folk art is usually classed by object-type rather than by either style or theme makes entertaining reading but neglects a basic ingredient: folk art's relationship to other traditions. At a certain stage in cultural awareness—one which we have surely reached by now—these relationships can be observed without in any way diminishing the high regard and delight we continue to have for these images. It would be interesting and useful to know if any mid-nineteenth-century American equestrian statues stand between *Buffalo Bill* and his most ancient source, Marcus Aurelius. There is a well-known Lion Killer weather vane at Shelburne with an image that can be related to both Delacroix and Rubens. Horse-and-sulky weather vanes should be studied in relation to the widely circulated prints of Currier and Ives, just as the prints themselves need to be carefully examined in relationship to European sources. It will not detract from the charm and integrity of the late nineteenth-century copper vane of Admiral Farragut to note that there is a distinct relationship to the great memorial executed by Saint Gaudens and erected in Madison Square in 1881.[20] Rather, in studying the resemblances between the two, one might arrive at a better, and surely a richer, idea of the accomplishments of the anonymous maker of the *Sea Captain*. An entire range of possibilities exists, worthy of serious exploration, but it must begin with careful comparison of the works.

If we begin to study folk art's styles and themes, influences will no doubt be found to flow both ways, not merely from high to folk. Doubtless the dates on many folk carvings will be changed, and our admiration for the ingenuity of the carvers may even increase when we realize the specific choices and conscious changes wrought in famous contemporary images. The relationship between, for example, the white-painted wood *Personification of Time*, dated 1825–40, and the Victory figure in Saint Gaudens's *General William Tecumseh Sherman* (1900) is too provocative to go unnoticed.[21] The folk carving is thought to personify Time because of the hourglass held in her raised right hand, the hand that in the Victory figure only gestures "Make way!" Was the folk figure destined to decorate a hearse, as Bishop suggests? Since her left hand carries the palm of victory that is also present in Saint Gaudens's work, might not the carver have wished to indicate victory over death? Furthermore, the essential movement of both figures is too pronounced not to suggest a fundamental formal relationship. It may be, of course, that both figures go to the same, as yet unidentified source. It seems more likely, however, that the folk piece is misdated by some sixty years and is a very sophisticated adaptation of the Saint Gaudens. One thing is visually certain: *Personification of Time* was not carved by a naive artisan cut off from the tradition of high art.

When we turn to more recent folk sculpture, the problems are even more complex. In the years following the Newark Museum's famous 1931 exhibition, there was a positive flurry of discovery of naive painters, native Henri Rousseaus.[22] This was capped, perhaps, by Sidney Janis's remarkable activity in 1942, not only in the

Far left: The Black Slave figure (1800–1820), with its remarkably classical proportions, was probably a trade sign for a slave auction. It was found in New Orleans, Louisiana. Painted wood with human teeth and glass eyes, height 56″. *The Marvill Collection.*

Below: Buffalo Bill Cody did much to create the taste for things western as he toured the country with his Wild West Show. Pennsylvania or Ohio, 1880–90. Painted wood, height 23¾″. *Heritage Plantation.*

exhibitions he organized but also by his book *They Taught Themselves.*[23] Perhaps inspired by serious studies of Rousseau's life,[24] an attempt was made to distinguish a category of artists somewhat different from "folk." Certain artists were called "popular"[25] when it became increasingly difficult for art to be produced anonymously and theoretically impossible for any such production to be reabsorbed into the environment. The whole environment, having become critically self-conscious, could no longer reabsorb what had been discovered, set aside for aesthetic value, and finally bought and sold and exhibited in a context of high art. One need only look at the case of Grandma Moses to realize the problem. "The tradition she, a naive artist, wished to join was much closer to her own vision [than Seraphine, Adolf Dietrich, or Rousseau, whose vision was linked with academic realism] but it was a folk tradition, already somewhat contaminated, and she herself was aesthetically self-conscious."[26]

In 1975, it is doubtful whether any folk tradition as Goldwater described is left, even slightly contaminated. With the post-war boom in communications and media interest, is it possible that there are any Folk left in America? Are any individuals or communities isolated or even insulated from a general culture? The manufacture and circulation of images through photographs, movies, television, and advertisements have only made technically complete what the massive discovery of folk art made a theoretical certainty as early as 1930. Mass communications have been so enormously productive of images that, by both quantity and electronic technique, they are literally reabsorbed in the invisibility of time, thus fulfilling on an unimagined scale and pace a primary condition of folk art. The images produced are anonymous because so omnipresent, understood—certainly!—and reabsorbed because consciously forgotten in their overwhelming succession. Some artists—high artists like Roy Lichtenstein—have grasped the possibility that they could be artists for all the people. Lichtenstein most valiantly and wittily created the famous original color print cover of Robert Kennedy for *Time.*[27] But this is the deliberate result of the often wished for, but seldom achieved, juncture of high art and popular interest. It is in no way an aspect of a cultural subset, as were the Shakers, Pennsylvania Dutch, different tribes of American Indians, or the Southwestern makers of *santos*.

The effort to persuade us that there is a true folk art today not only ignores the primary conditions of the transmission of visual ideas since at least 1950 but, by omission, makes a folk hero out of anyone who can resist the flood of material. But the artist who can take such material and invest it with civilized meaning, in the tradition of great and always selfconscious art, belongs to high art, even though he may deserve to be a hero of the people. Those who would see a modern folk art—apart from Lichtenstein, Johns, Warhol, Dine—still springing from "the organic nature of things" practice, in a quasi-refined manner, the discovery of found objects.

Duchamp's presentation of found objects had its initial 1913-15 impetus in his realization of the ironic consequences of the separation of content from pure form that grew among artists and their defenders early in our century. The democratic idea of making each collector an artist and each artist a collector parallels the slowly emerging consciousness that photography is art rather than mere reportage or an objective record of reality. Thus it is not accidental that much of the presentation of so-called contemporary folk art, or grass-roots art, or outsider art, consists of photo documentation of parts of extinct (destroyed) architectural/sculptural environments such as the one created by Clarence Schmidt at Woodstock, New York—an artists' colony since World War I. As Schmidt constructed his private vision, so it must be discovered by someone endowed with the capacity to find, to see its value, and to impose that vision on a willing part of society, the vastly enlarged community receptive to art.

All that is lacking in this attractive and genuinely moving effort is the similar discovery of the source behind the found object, a discovery complicated by the realities and techniques of visual information transmission. In the last twenty years, more people have seen a shadow of Michelangelo's accomplishment on the Sistine ceiling than all the people who have lived since its creation. When we confront recently created objects of folk art, we may admire the objects, admire even more the artist's urge to pursue obsessively his vision for years and years. We should also admire the complex process of cultural diffusion that joins the isolated, untaught, or self-taught artist to the images and ideas of aesthetic innovators—the artists, past and present, who invented the images whose effectiveness is proven by the manner in which they reach these relatively innocent Folk.

Can it be true that there are artists who "if they visit museums and enjoy the works . . . are not actually inspired by them" for the "restrictions of their lives leave them pure to paint (or carve) with total honesty . . ."?[28] Total honesty is something that seekers of high art periodically search for. Perhaps they seek it in particularly simplistic terms when the techniques and meanings of those who invent images become so precious or ingrown

22

Below: The way in which the joints of this figure in a tin cap (*circa* 1920) are articulated indicates that it was originally joined to a crank mechanism that propelled it in a rocking motion. Painted wood and tin with marble eyes, height 43¾″. *Robert Bishop*.

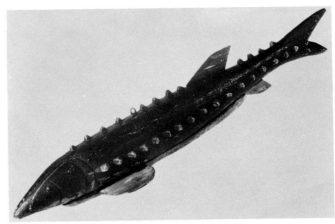

Above: Sturgeon Fish Decoy, Wisconsin, 20th century. Painted wood and tin, length 29″. *Robert Bishop*.

Below: This horse was originally a trade sign for a blacksmith shop. Wood with metal horseshoes and leather ears, height 34¼″. *The Barenholz Collection*.

23

24

Left: The figure of a kneeling sailor shown here was made as the base for a ship's chart table in the early 19th century. The head was originally flat. Salem, Massachusetts. Painted wood, height 27". *From the Smithsonian Institution, National Museum of History and Technology, Eleanor and Mabel Van Alstyne American Folk Art Collection.*

Top right: Abraham Lincoln is probably the favorite political hero of the folk artist, surpassing even George Washington in popularity. This bust, a centennial commemoration of Lincoln's birth, has "C O" and "Feb. 5 (?) 1908" incised on the base. Painted wood, height 18". *Mr. and Mrs. Bertram K. Little.*

Bottom right: George Washington on his charger, Jack, was one of the many images of Washington that flourished in the 19th century. The theme was made familiar through popular engravings. The carving shown here (*circa* 1845) was found in the vicinity of the Ohio-Pennsylvania border near Pittsburgh. Painted wood, height 13⅞". *Private Collection.*

25

Left: Medicine Man, probably Pennsylvania, *circa* 1850. Painted pine with tin and taxidermist eyes, height 21⅞″. *Abby Aldrich Rockefeller Folk Art Collection.*

Below: Seated Man with Derby, found in southern Ohio, *circa* 1870. Wood, height 19″. *George E. Schoellkopf Gallery.*

26

that a fragment of audience sets out on a deliberate pilgrimage to find signs of art's enduring power and universality. In their finding, often powered by a belief that they are as sensitive and gifted as those whose creativity proclaims them artists, the process of selection itself has, of course, created the art form. Nonetheless, in every case there is the genuine effort on the part of the discovered artist (whether named or anonymous) to place between himself and his experience of life a "whole set of conventions, inhibitions, and acquired experiences." Robert Herbert wrote that "an artist cannot suddenly make up his mind to render what he sees and feels, for these acts are not neutral, nor simply acts of will and technique."[29] Every work of art, whether sophisticated or naive, involves the art of choosing. In the past, we have accepted the capacity of human intelligence to be effectively self-taught in literature, philosophy, or other primarily verbal disciplines. In our contemporary world, with its wealth of readily available visual history, can we assume that the self-taught artist must be naive? That his choices are untutored or unconscious? That his intuition has not been filtered through both visual and verbal exposure or through intelligence?

Perhaps, without condescending, it is possible to find objects, buildings, whole environments constructed by artists who create with a large measure of intuition. But it is not possible to deny the operation of tradition, and the operative tradition three-quarters of the way through the present century is wholly in the self-consciousness of high art and its fascination, long ago played out, with non-culture. The discovery of often bizarre curiosities, so full of poetry, love, and history, sometimes so redolent of a tradition's decay, is an extension of the found object. That many contemporary or recent folk sculptors are discovered in towns like Taos, or Woodstock (Clarence Schmidt), or Springs (Albert Price) is a double function of the self-taught artist to be instructed and stimulated by his environment and to be "found" by the searchers in such colonies.

More interesting and pathetic is the occasional survival of a genuine, if faint, trace of what was once a continuous and separable tradition, such as Kachina dolls. By 1930 Kachina dolls were already reduced to the level of a tourist art, despite several attempted revivals by anthropologists beginning at the turn of the century. A Mickey Mouse Kachina,[30] although not without charm and rife with social implications, is a travesty of both Kachina tradition and Walt Disney. Faced with an abundance of identifiable images, the contemporary connoisseur of folk art must wonder how the artist came to encounter the art he is copying; he must wonder what

27

Woman with Tambourine was made by Ed Davis in 1935. It is similar to the work of Elie Nadelman, who was one of the first artists to collect and be influenced by American folk art. Painted wood with metal and pearl earrings, height 17″. *Herbert W. Hemphill, Jr.*

Left: The Bathing Beauty (1973) was made by Clarence Stringfield, who was born in Erin, West Virginia, in 1903. He was a farmer and cabinetmaking instructor until the 1930's, when he was bedridden for a year with tuberculosis and began carving. Although he keeps busy with several kinds of shop work—replacing gunstocks, filing saws, repairing musical instruments, metalworking—his carving tools are quite simple: jackknife, pocketknife, and chisels. He is also a fiddler, and carved his fiddle himself. Nashville, Tennessee. Painted wood, height 57½″. *Estelle Friedman.*

Opposite: This figure of a devout Jew surrounded by his holy books and ritual objects was carved out of a log found in Prospect Park, Brooklyn, New York. The artist, Frank Mazur (b. 1910), calls it *For Your Faith to Survive You Must Live It.* 1974. Wood, height 56″. *Lent by the Artist.*

moving relationship established a connection with visual material that led a man or woman to seek to place himself in that tradition.

Often the most arresting quality of the objects themselves is their medium and technique, sometimes as ingenious as the construction of a car sculpture entirely from bottle caps[31] or a human toastmaster, related to the traditional figure of Uncle Sam, from tin cans. These bespeak the degree of sophistication of the maker and reveal the obsession of the hobbiest. But the forms themselves, and less often the techniques, bear a complex relationship to the forms of high and commercial art. The iconography of the most ambitious groups frequently reaches back to Christian themes that found their apogee in art prior to the nineteenth century. Why, one must wonder, is our more isolated nineteenth-century folk sculpture more secular than that of recent years? Perhaps the answer lies in the ready availability of reproductions of sixteenth-century paintings. Patrocina Barela, who carved so many biblical scenes with a pocket knife before his death in Taos in 1964, may never have learned to read or write, but he clearly knew how to look at pictures. He knew also how to distinguish the famous from the less renowned: his *Expulsion from the Garden* is derived from Michelangelo's *Fall of Man* on the Sistine ceiling.[32]

And what is the role of conscious irony in these presumably untutored works? Would Clarence Stringfield's 1973 *Bathing Beauty* have been "found" had it been called Lady Wrestler? Would Jesse Howards's 1967 *Snow Shovel* have been found so interesting had Marcel Duchamp not found *his* snow shovel in 1915? We see a 1971 copy of Titian's *Rape of Europa* by a forty-eight-year-old prisoner; we see Angela Palladino, whose *Nude in the Grass*, 1967, is as much in debt to Matisse as ever was Max Weber; we see Frank Mazur, a highly individual pupil of Toshio Odate, but still a pupil; or "Driftwood" Charlie Kisling deriving his inspiration knowingly from pre-Columbian art, Mayan or Peruvian, imitating even the texture of volcanic tufa.[33] The common thread through all of these current derivations is the staggering range of available visual material and the total lack of a continuously operating tradition in so-called contemporary folk art. There can be no continuously operating tradition in a culture without Folk.

Folk sculpture and painting in a culture without Folk is selected by some collectors primarily on the basis of its irrelevance to or removal from the primary conditions or sensations of modern life. It is for this reason that anachronistic subjects, such as the religious parodies of Tolson or Miles Carpenter, are favored. Conversely, the strange marriages of high art themes with hobbiest

29

techniques appeal to a sophisticated jaded taste in a way that may or may not have been intended by the artist. (The more intentional the strange union, the less Folk the artist.) Among the many influences and relationships that have contributed to the formation of American folk art, we—collectors, dealers, curators, or historians—must add our own influence. Its cumulative effect all too frequently crosses the thin line separating patronage from corruption in modern society. It governs by both selection (which is remedial) and by influencing production (which is not), subsuming the folk roots of a tradition. Too often, meaning is submerged or discounted by formal values and our very appreciation (often profoundly condescending) permanently transforms not only the society from which Folk once emerged but the artifacts that were moving evidence of their existence.

1 Edwin Alden Jewell, "American Primitives," *New York Times*, September 27, 1931.

2 "Africa," *New York Times*, April 15, 1923.

3 See an interesting exchange between Robert Macbeth and Alfred H. Barr, Jr., in "Art Notes," *New York Times*, March 22, 1931.

4 Robert Goldwater, *Primitivism in Modern Art*, rev. ed. (New York: Vintage Books, 1967). Cited as Goldwater, 1967.

5 Robert Bishop, *American Folk Sculpture* (New York: E. P. Dutton & Co., 1974). Cited as Bishop, 1974; Herbert W. Hemphill, Jr., and Julia Weissman, *Twentieth-Century American Folk Art and Artists* (New York: E. P. Dutton & Co., 1974). Cited as Hemphill and Weissman, 1974; and Jean Lipman, *Provocative Parallels: Naive Early American/International Sophisticates* (New York: E. P. Dutton & Co., 1975).

6 Hemphill and Weissman, 1974, pp. 9, 10.

7 John T. Kirk, *Early American Furniture* (New York: Alfred A. Knopf, 1970); and John T. Kirk, *American Chairs: Queen Anne and Chippendale* (New York: Alfred A. Knopf, 1972).

8 One practical, although partial answer is found in the reluctance of most scholarly institutions to recognize the aesthetic quality of folk art, to encourage it as a valid subject for scholars.

9 Robert Goldwater, "An Approach to African Sculpture," *Parnassus*, May 1935.

10 Goldwater, 1967, p. 185, citing Zervos's observation that Rousseau's work was not truly popular because it was not the product of a collective conscience.

11 Goldwater, 1967, pp. 178–92, esp. 185–90.

12 See, for example, Louise Gebhard Gann, "An Artist of the People," *International Studio*, July 1925.

13 See Dora Vallier, *Henri Rousseau* (Cologne, 1961); and Henri Certigny, *La Verite sur Le Douanier Rousseau* (Paris, 1961).

14 In "An Artist of the People" Gann said that "the craftsmen of the middle ages may have been his [Rousseau's] precursors, but he is the sole modern artist in whom there is no eclecticism, no influence. He is primitive in the sense that he is himself—isolated and ignorant."

15 See Chicago, Illinois, Renaissance Society at the University of Chicago, *Modern Primitives*, 1931, by James Johnson Sweeney; and E. A. Jewell, "Modern Primitives in Renaissance Society Hall," *New York Times*, July 29, 1931.

16 Holger Cahill described folk sculpture as "an expression of the common people, and not of a small cultured class. Folk art usually has not much to do with the fashionable art of its period. It is never the product of art movements, but comes out of craft traditions plus that personal something of the rare craftsman who is an artist by nature if not by training. This art is not based on measurement or calculation but on feeling, and it rarely fits in with standards of realism. It goes straight to the fundamentals of art, rhythm, design, balance, proportion, which the folk artist feels instinctively" (Newark, New Jersey, Newark Museum, *Folk Sculpture*, October 1931).

17 Edwin Alden Jewell, "American Primitives," *New York Times*, October 25, 1931.

18 Carl Zigrosser, Robert Harshe, Julianna Force, E. A. Jewell, Douglas Haskell, B. D. Saklatwalla, Stephen Bourgeois, Guy Pène du Bois, and Malcolm Vaughan, "American Renaissance," *Creative Art*, November 1931.

19 Hemphill and Weissman, 1974, pp. 10–11, in a discussion based on quotations from Sir Herbert Read, *Art and Society* (London: Schocken Books, 1966).

20 See Bishop, 1974, fig. 109; and Wayne Craven, *Sculpture in America* (New York: Thomas Y. Crowell Company, 1968), fig. 11.1. Cited as Craven, 1968.

21 Bishop, 1974, fig. 52; and Craven, 1968, fig. 11.6.

22 An article that slightly preceded the exhibition is a valuable reminder of the atmosphere of discovery in 1930 compared with that of 1975. "Many Americans have felt how sad it is that . . . the soul of our people cannot produce even the modest blossom of folk expression. They have become used to the idea that art, especially folk art, is something that flourishes only in far countries and that at home it is a dry stalk. But folk art has been produced in America for 200 years and more. It is being produced today, though on a rather small scale" (Holger Cahill, "Folk Art," *American Mercury*, September 1931).

23 Sidney Janis, *They Taught Themselves* (New York: Dial, 1942).

24 Christian Zervos, *Rousseau* (Paris, 1927), and Wilhelm Uhde, "Henri Rousseau et les Primitifs Modernes," *L'Amour de l'Art* 14, 1933.

25 See especially New York, New York, Museum of Modern Art, *Masters of Popular Painting: Modern Primitives of Europe and America*, 1932.

26 Goldwater, 1967, p. 190.

27 See Cambridge, Massachusetts, Fogg Art Museum, *The Graphic Art of Roy Lichtenstein*, 1975, by Henri Zerner, pp. 4, 13–14.

28 Hemphill and Weissman, 1974, p. 18.

29 Boston, Museum of Fine Arts, *Barbizon Revisited*, 1962, essay and catalogue by Robert Herbert, p. 13.

30 Hemphill and Weissman, 1974, p. 89. The Mickey Mouse Kachina is dated 1925 by Hemphill, but would seem to require a later date, since the first short Mickey Mouse cartoons came out in 1928.

31 Hemphill and Weissman, 1974, fig. 29.

32 Hemphill and Weissman, 1974, p. 126; and Frederick Hartt, *Michelangelo* (New York: Harry N. Abrams, 1965).

33 See Hemphill and Weissman, 1974, figs. 246, 251, 262, 296, 147, 146.

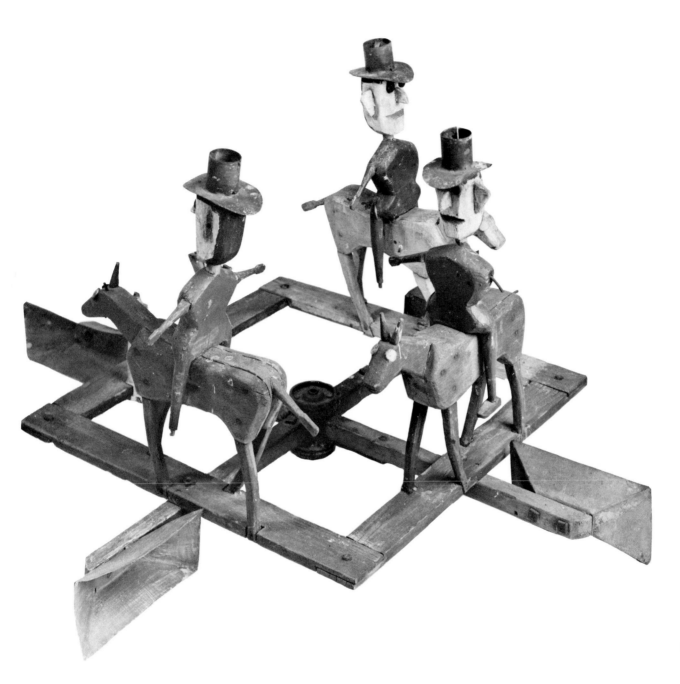

When activated by wind, the movement
of the four horsemen (one is missing) of
this late 19th-century whirligig produced
an effect like animated film. Ohio.
Painted wood and metal, height 15½″,
width 29″. *Herbert W. Hemphill, Jr.*

32

A Sorting Process: The artist as collector

A conversation between Sarah Faunce, Curator of Paintings and Sculpture, The Brooklyn Museum, and Michael D. Hall, Sculptor

New York, 1975

Above: Reportedly from South Carolina, this is one of two known examples of turtle decoys. It was probably made early in the 20th century. Painted wood, length 29". *Collection of Michael and Julie Hall.*

Left: The Buckeye Family (*circa* 1925) is the only known work by Joe Lee (d. 1941), a greengrocer from Beaverhill, Tennessee. Legend has it that he took up carving after having successfully "improved" a small boy's carved wooden doll. He completed the Buckeye Family, a work which attracted much critical attention, in three years. Painted wood, height of man 56". *The Barbara Johnson Collection.*

Faunce What I want to start with is really what interests me most and has since I saw the pictures of your collection and knew who you were—the fact that you are a contemporary, sophisticated sculptor coming to your maturity in the 60's, and at the same time you are a connoisseur of this naive tradition. I am interested in how you and Julie got involved with folk sculpture.

Hall Of course, that seems to be the first question that everybody comes up with. Where does it all tie in? I think all too often they want a very pat sort of correlation, one-to-one.

SF Which is impossible.

MH Well, there are certainly connections. In this instance, vis-à-vis my work and the interest in collecting American folk art, I can't really clarify it through a direct sort of path. It's rather obscure, even to me. However, folk art is meaningful to me and as long as it's meaningful, I trust it to be reliable. It has really more to do with an attitude and has more to do with an outlook than it has to do with forms.

For thirty-five or forty years now we have seen artists in sequence, contemporary artists, trying to build off a base that embraces this material. Nadelman being the key example, moving right on down to someone like William King, Red Grooms, Marisol—all those names. We find them tying into a folk art tradition in the sense of finding an inspiration in forms, and we see that manifest in the work. If you can't go cause and effect, you can at least go mood and interpretation, style and variation of a theme. And these things go directly into a look. Not so in my work. It will never be.

SF That's why the question. You know, with Marisol, for instance, you can almost feel . . . see . . . a one-to-one connection.

MH I think what is meaningful is that I was born in California. I had that rootless sort of West Coast identity, a product of the post-war period when my family moved out there, as many people did. I was born into a world where history was the last five minutes. It was quite an eye-opener to move east. I went to Colorado. Then I moved to Kentucky, where I taught at the university and met Bert Hemphill in the mid-60's. And all of a sudden, some kind of connection to a history—a cultural history—seemed to fascinate me. Then to find it in these

Man with the Pony,
Campton, Kentucky,
circa 1950.
Edgar Tolson
(b. 1904). Painted
wood, height 23¼″.
*Collection of
Michael and
Julie Hall.*

objects, which I perceived as beautiful, made it very intriguing. I had that great sense that I could simply declare my roots. I didn't have to be from some New England family and know that a particular group of portraits was my birthright. I could just say, "This is my birthright." I elected my birthright rather than having to find it in a family or find it in a subculture or find it in an environment. That was exciting.

As an artist, I think that the same kind of arbitrary, very free approach to finding an aesthetic family tree carried right over into what I think about my own work. My childhood was without art in every sense, so when I came to art I could pick my parentage, as it were. If David Smith made sense to me, then David Smith could be plugged into my ancestor tree, right? If Mark Di Suvero made sense to me, I could plug him in.

Not necessarily by choice but certainly by circumstance, I have been in the American Midwest now for almost nine years. And all of those clichés—the bread basket, Middle America, all of that business—came home to me very dramatically. Folk art is tied to the land. It's tied to a sense of self. It's tied to regions. They're all manifest in folk art. That has become interesting to me. The value of folk art may be in its affirmation of the self in the very individual sense, in the local sense of a community, in the regional sense of maybe an ethnic group or a locale, and then, of course, in the final analysis, in the national sense—that quality of being an American. I was looking for an American identity. The work made sense to me that way.

Julie and I found Edgar Tolson in the mountains of Kentucky. Okay, here's a fine artist and he is Edgar Tolson and his work is so terribly limited. Maybe this is a digression, but I remember sitting in the house one evening and a young artist from California was talking to me. After about five gin and tonics, he looked over at one of Tolson's pieces and said, "Michael, I have got to tell you, that's the most limited thing I've ever seen." And through the fog, it was suddenly very clear. He was absolutely right. That was the magnificence of it. It was so terribly limited that it *mattered*. Because it was Tolson's limitation and nobody else's that brought that thing into existence. And it therefore stood for Tolson and Tolson stood for it and neither could be removed. Culture in the sense of us, the we, that affirmation of a time and a place, and a people was the poorer without it. And then it occurred to me that Michelangelo was also limited, terribly limited in the same way. The Pope notwithstanding, you see. Without the limitation, he didn't matter, but with it he mattered terribly.

And all of a sudden, I understood my own art and understood why folk art spoke to me. I saw that the vocabulary that I was looking at in the folk art material was what I call the "one man, one pocket knife" statement, which is not the factory cigar store Indian, is not factory decoys, is not carousel horses. I'm talking about the kind of material that this show is about, where you find that affirmation of self, "I am," reiterated again and again. When it's done with that much authority or that awesome confidence, indeed you *are*—it finally matters. When it finally becomes poetic and it finally becomes not replaceable, not interchangeable with anything else you have experienced, ever, then it's all there is. That's my definition of culture, a collective compilation of that.

SF Absolutely authentic. Someone like Tolson makes these things because he is Tolson and he has to make them.

MH Absolutely. And that he *did* make them matters. His existence on this earth somehow is validated right there. In a sense we need him to know who we are. We need that he is to believe that we are.

Some of the latest theory in anthropology is really starting to come to grips with this as a notion about what it is that demarcates humanness or humanity. Jane Goodall has pretty well destroyed the notion that tool-making per se is the line of demarcation. It's proven that the apes make tools, use tools.

SF And, of course, now they're talking; or, at least, there are all those experiments with language.

MH And so others are suggesting—of course, it's yet to be tested in the philosophical and clinical arenas where these kinds of things are tested—that it might be man's ability to make art or his need to make art or the fact that he makes art that is the initial cut above which you finally have humankind versus animalkind.

And that brings you down to the question of the definition of art. The definition that I'm using really has to do with the declaration of self or the recognition of self in time. This could be manifested in a cave painting when you could finally depict your tribe in the midst of a bison hunt. That afternoon, that particular event. Or maybe the depiction is in terms of wish fulfillment: that season when you needed the good hunt. The content of the cave painting doesn't matter. What matters is the fact that the cave painting finally said that a man recognized that he existed and recognized that he existed within a context—his tribe, the seasons, the environment, the interaction with nature, the herd of bison—and he recorded his awareness. That he was finally moved to state his existence made him man.

The folk artist does that. He does that for us. In my opinion, the fine artist also does that and does that for

35

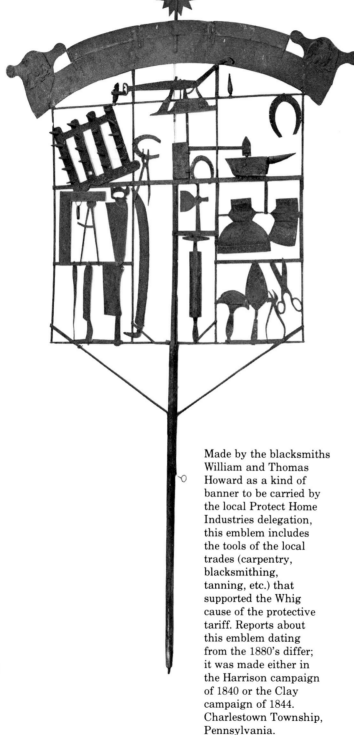

Made by the blacksmiths William and Thomas Howard as a kind of banner to be carried by the local Protect Home Industries delegation, this emblem includes the tools of the local trades (carpentry, blacksmithing, tanning, etc.) that supported the Whig cause of the protective tariff. Reports about this emblem dating from the 1880's differ; it was made either in the Harrison campaign of 1840 or the Clay campaign of 1844. Charlestown Township, Pennsylvania. Painted iron and tin, height 9'10". *Chester County Historical Society.*

us—I'm talking collectively about us as a people or as humankind. That's why there's always going to be art. Every generation has to have its artists. They affirm our existence for us, though we don't always accept their art. That's always the problem, of course. Art and art history; art and art criticism; art and style; art and taste; art and acceptance; art and alienation. All that business. It doesn't matter. It goes on. In the sophisticated scene we try to have some understanding of the criteria and we find artists bound together with a kind of recognition of them. We find the dealer system and museums behind them in the sense of trying to affirm or confirm them. The folk artist is doing it anyway. That's really the only difference. He just hasn't been brought into the embrace. Who's to know how long that situation will really continue. A lot of the contemporary folk artists now are being clutched to our cultural breast almost to the point of suffocation. Almost from the day after they're discovered under the rock where they're working quietly. But that's because they matter, you see. Tolson matters. He is a national treasure and what he does for himself, for his family, for the people of his town, for the people of eastern Kentucky, for the people of the South, and for the people of the nation, in its own small way, matters. I don't think I'm overextending this. He is one among many. He happens to be so very good, and when they get that good, they matter more and more. When I classify him as a national treasure, I guess I'm utilizing personal criteria and trying to fit them into a concept that's essentially not very widespread in this country. In Japan it's very common to tap people for recognition and ascendancy to public confirmation.

SF You mean the Japanese tradition of designating an artist a Living National Treasure?

MH Yes. That's the way I see Tolson and that's who I would like to be and that's where it ties in.

SF I had a number of questions about how you relate to this kind of unsophisticated material as a sophisticated artist. I was looking at some pictures of your work—big, structural statements that retain a very country feeling. I wondered if that was a feeling at all connected with the folk sculpture.

MH Well, no. I think that quality of something country or countrified in my work is again . . .

SF By country, I don't mean quaint. I mean something that is built out of the ground, that relates to the ground.

MH Well, that's true. They're for landscape. They're conceived in that sort of space—the space I inhabit, which isn't urban space. It's not a rural space, but it's a different kind of skyline and a different kind of source—

Detroit or Kentucky—where I have worked. So my work relates to folk art indirectly, through my recognition of the fact that the folk artist always works out of his limits. He never questions that what he does might be otherwise. His sources are always personal or, at most, local. That's what gives his work its quality. That's what gives it its character. For too long we have felt condescending about this. It's seemed somehow provincial—a damning label to set on any work of art, because provincial suggests . . .

SF . . . That it's not aware of the whole tradition of art.

MH Right. You start to believe that the art world begins and ends in Soho or uptown—the galleries. And it's not so. Soho itself is a province, you see. It's quite possible that the work that comes out of there is provincial, that it comes out of a very local value. That that value is hyped to become the art world is another problem altogether. But I think it's perfectly reasonable that somebody working in New York would be involved with a New York value, with images that come out of a New York environment and a contact and a stimulation—the New York view.

I am obviously not provincial. However, my work might come out of a personal value or local source. It's not only reasonable, but maybe the only way it can grow. And that again is something I get from this material. It's a stabilizing sort of view. I'm not trying to make folk art. I'm not trying to make selfconsciously provincial or regional things. My work is cognizant. But that it would flow from me is terribly important to me. And if it finally matters, it will be because I matter. Without that, it wouldn't be about anything anyway.

I live in the midst of a houseful of folk art that affirms my existence for me, that becomes a buffer against all the confusions that can beset me. I'm trying to work, trying to be an artist in today's world and still know what I know and see what I've seen and value what I value. Folk sculpture, in my dark moments, is a certain solace to me. I can look at Edgar Tolson's work and know that it matters. It's the work's validity that's so important to me. If I can live with enough valid things that come from a solid base, where there are no extenuating circumstances, they become a monitor or check on what I do in the studio myself. I have to walk through the collection to get to the studio and it becomes an eerie sort of gauntlet. They stand there and tell me what my mission really is. To come back from work, to have to pass through their scrutiny again, where the ideas that I've just set forth, the image I've just created, and the value that I've just made manifest—whatever it is that I've just formulated in the

Whirligig Weather Vane, Southern Ohio, 1880–1900. Wood, length 40¼". *Collection of Michael and Julie Hall.*

The Girl on a Pig (*circa* 1910) was originally part of a waterwheel-operated whirligig of some forty almost life-size articulated figures. Clark Coe built it to amuse his crippled nephew who, when orphaned, had come to live with him in Killingworth, Connecticut. Painted wood with metal, horsehair, and ribbon, height 34¾". *Herbert W. Hemphill, Jr.*

37

Indian Squaw and Scout, New Jersey (?), *circa* 1870.
Painted and stained wood, height 48½″ and 62″.
Herbert W. Hemphill, Jr.

studio—has to stand a comparative test. And I don't live with inferior things. I want the best. The better they are, the harder they are on me, which I think is good. I like the discipline, I like the challenge.

I could walk through a room with three or four David Smiths or a Mark Di Suvero or a Peter Voulkos and feel the same kind of thing. And I wouldn't separate it. If I could own the Smiths, I would have them too. I find the identity and value in Smith's work fantastic. I can sense that "one man, one pocket knife" quality running through his things, even though he works in welded steel materials. They can stand next to those black figures of ours, and the black figures can stand next to David Smith. They're not the same in appearance, but in terms of what they confirm about art, they are very, very similar for me.

In terms of where I came from, what I'm looking for, and what I'm requiring of myself right now, it's been very positive to be in the midst of folk art. All the other qualities are there, too—that charm and fascination, the sense of time, the variety in this material, the images themselves. And, of course, who doesn't love all the patina and humor in some of it? It's all there. I've developed a taste for it.

SF In Tolson's *Fall of Man* series the humor is somehow irresistible.

MH I don't think it's a humorous piece.

SF By humor I don't mean laughable. I mean the simplicity and the literalness of the images.

MH Well, there's a lot of clarity in the piece. I have my own notions about that piece. I have lived with it long enough to have the feeling that he's really giving us something terribly profound in terms of the content and something very reductive, very essential in terms of the handling. That's why the piece is as successful as it is. It's really a self-portrait. It's really his own comment on the personal isolation of the individual soul in this life. It begins with a blissful situation of conviviality, right? And then progressively moves, or sequentially moves, to a state of isolation—that Cain figure standing in the last tableau staring off into nowhere, somehow having survived birth and death, alone. The sorrow that's so clear in the Eve figure bent over the fallen brother is one of the facts of life. Tolson acknowledges most of the facts of life through that whole set-up. Yet he also acknowledges the indomitable quality of a man. Tolson himself, in a way. Man's destiny is what really comes through in the piece.

Edgar Tolson is a great artist and Edgar Tolson makes his best statement for me in the single figures he carves. I've seen dozens of them and they always have that frozen frontality that's so in-turned, almost Gothic.

It's reserved, it's enigmatic. It's sad, in a way, and yet it's profoundly under control, stoic. There's an amount of compassion in it. All in those single figures. The Appalachians call them dolls. But they are all autobiographical. They look straight ahead and their arms, 90 percent of the time, are held right at their sides. They have that kind of visage where you don't penetrate beyond the mask, the appearance of the face. The man inside is closed to you. As most Appalachians are closed to outsiders. As they are closed to their own families.

SF Really not communicative.

MH Not really. It's a subcultural kind of view. It's the thing that everyone always stereotypes: the suspicious, reactionary, southern Appalachian who would just as soon shoot you as look at you. We've heard all those clichés. But those characteristics grow out of the isolation of those pockets, those little hollows up there where they live, facing a world where they are essentially outcast, as are Eskimos and so many other poor subculture groups. Their view now is almost endemic. It's right there. And I see Tolson so very aware of it because he lives it every day. He has lived it every day for seventy years and he has become its poet laureate. He can say it and he can say it so well.

So the charm in the *Fall of Man* series is superficial. There's something else you're seeing. Tolson is taking you through life as he has felt it and life as he knows it to be, which is from paradise to expulsion, integration to alienation. The conjunction, which is ideal, then the disruptions, which are actual, are the givens in the equation of Appalachian life. There is a sense of forebearance, you know, that it will go on anyway, which is a very strange thing to live with. It is acknowledged in the single figure—Tolson, to me—in that last set-up. The space between the Cain figure and the weeping Eve is such a significant space. Merce Cunningham doesn't organize space any better. This is where the question of what is sophisticated and what is not gets to be a moot point. I've lived with that piece for close to six years. It's right upstairs and I move through it visually. Just in the last year or so I've started to find this other level in it. It's very real. I think anyone who sees the piece in the exhibition will feel its reality. He'll start to understand the space and start to feel the psychological relationships between the dolls and start to understand how Tolson really sees it. I could talk about each piece in the group, but it's not as important as to know that it begins perfect, in tune with itself, and ends perfect again (or imperfect, depending on your view), but out of phase with itself. It ends with actualities rather than ideals. Those people live a very actual life and Tolson's really

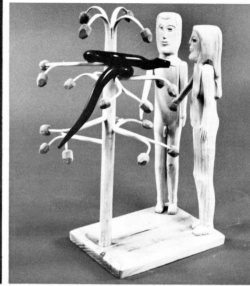

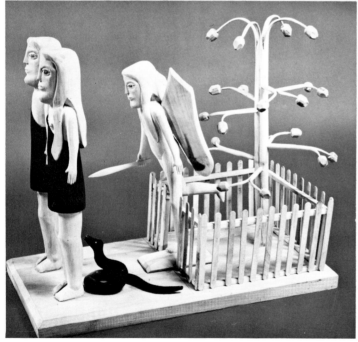

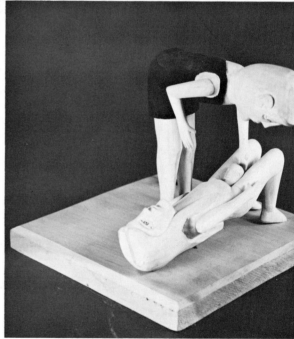

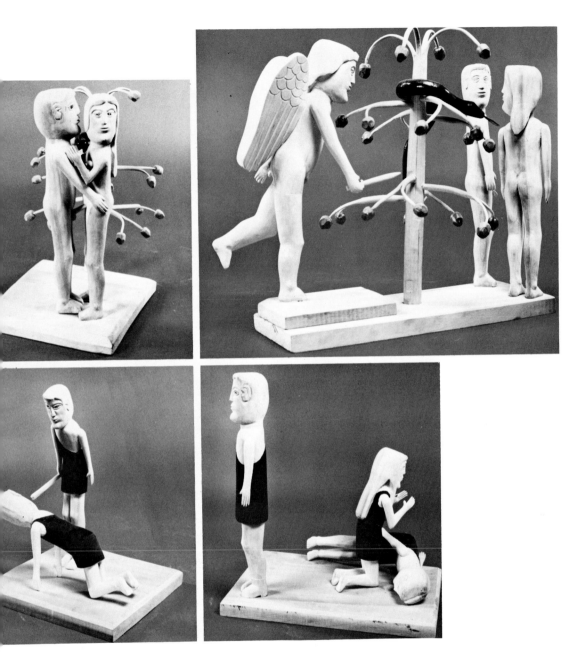

Edgar Tolson was born in Lee City, Kentucky, in 1904. Educated through the 6th grade, he has been married twice and is the father of eighteen children.

A descendant of 17th-century settlers of English origin, he is a hard-drinking, tobacco-chewing, story-telling philosopher of Campton, Kentucky, where he now lives. He calls himself a wood-carver now, but he has been a preacher, farmer, cobbler, cabinetmaker, and itinerant worker. He has been carving for over thirty-five years, sometimes in stone but usually in wood. He has carved several versions of the Paradise/Expulsion theme as single pieces, but the Cain and Abel story exists only in this set of eight painted wood scenes.

From left to right, the Fall of Man is shown by: *top*: Paradise (height 12½″), Temptation (height 15½″), Original Sin (height 14½″), Expulsion (height 12½″); *bottom*: Paradise Barred (height 15½″), Birth of Cain (height 8″), Cain Slays Abel (height 13″), Cain Goes into the World (height 14½″). *Collection of Michael and Julie Hall.*

41

Miles B. Carpenter was born in Lancaster County,
Pennsylvania, in 1889. He opened a sawmill in 1912
in Waverly, Virginia, where he still lives. Carpenter
began his carvings purely for pleasure in 1940. Around
1955 he closed the mill and opened an icehouse and fruit
stand for which he carved a watermelon slice trade sign.
In 1963 he began to fill his pickup truck with remarkable
figures (some of which are illustrated here) and back it
to the roadside. He would sell these figures, some directly
off the truck, so the group was constantly changing.
This photograph gives some indication of the startling
impact of Carpenter's display.

Right: As Carpenter drove around the town, he would pull a string attached to this Indian's head; the warrior would turn and stare at passersby. 1967. Painted wood and fabric, height 67″. *Jeffrey T. Camp.*

Below: Root Monkey, 1967. Painted wood, height 30½″. *Jeffrey T. Camp.*

Bottom left: Watermelon Trade Sign, 1960. Painted wood with metal handcart, length of watermelon 39½″, length of handcart 38″. *Abby Aldrich Rockefeller Folk Art Collection.*

Bottom center: Root Bulldog, 1968. Painted wood, height 16″. *Lent by the Artist.*

Bottom right: Pumpkin in a Wheelbarrow, 1960. Painted wood, diameter of pumpkin 25″, length of wheelbarrow 6′. *Jeffrey T. Camp.*

43

The most recent information indicates that
this figure of Uncle Sam was carved from a
tree trunk in North Reading, Massachusetts,
in the mid-1930's. Painted pine, height 89¼".
Museum of Fine Arts, Boston.

telling you about that. It's directly out of his own
experience.

But he has none of these notions about it. I've talked
with him about his work—and you talk about sophisticated or unsophisticated. I asked him one time where
these things come from, and he said, "Michael, a person
that makes those things, if you could open up his skull
and look inside, you would see the piece there, perfect
as it's made. You don't make it with your hands. You
form it with your hands. You make it with your mind."
I defy anybody to find a more succinct insight into the
art process than that.

SF Oh, absolutely. And it goes right back to Michelangelo, for that matter—the whole Platonic idea.

MH Whatever. Artists of all kinds have always tried to
tell us this, and we have always tried to talk to them or
talk about them in terms of talent or facility, in terms of
hand-skill. Unimportant. Those things only serve, you
see. The forms themselves, the materials themselves, are
armatures only. Armatures for ideas. That an artist
needs to be able to articulate his idea with words is obviously not a requirement. Yet we always expect it. I'm
free when I deal with folk art; I don't expect it. I don't
have to. I can go through the work free, and if it's there, I
hope I can find it. It's a process of riddling out, puzzling
over. The business on Tolson's *Fall of Man* will be
challenged by a lot of people. They won't want to see it.
They'll think I'm off the mark, trying to read too much
into the series. They'll think I'm attributing . . .

SF . . . Projecting into it.

MH Yes, attributing a great deal to a source that's not
capable of these insights or capable of rendering these
complex notions or capable of grappling with this kind
of content in a work of art. I don't care. Go ahead. Take
issue with it and then go look at the piece. I'll say it here
and leave it for someone else to read. I'm not gushy and
I'm not sentimental about it and I don't have an axe to
grind. I look at folk art for my own reasons, and I find
what I find in it for my own reasons. You people want to
borrow some of what Julie and I live with to show other
people. Fine. And if you want to ask me about it, I'll tell
you what I think.

SF But you're not out to proselytize about it.

MH I'm not, no. I'm not messianic about it. I think that
American folk art at its best moments is terribly important, but any art is terribly important at its best
moments for reasons that I've already clarified. It's just
that, in my opinion, American folk art is one of those
very strange vocabularies that really haven't been understood critically yet. One of the reasons for this is that

The giant curlew weather vane (*circa* 1870), one of the largest known, once dominated the Cape May County Shooting and Gun Club in New Jersey. Sheet iron with gold leaf, length 92". *Mrs. Jacob M. Kaplan.*

Indian Rifleman Weather Vane, late 18th-early 19th century. Iron, height 31". *The Marvill Collection.*

Found on an Ohio barn, the size of the cockerel weather vane indicates the immense size of the building above which it once turned. Last half of the 19th century. Painted wood with metal straps, height 34". *Abby Aldrich Rockefeller Folk Art Collection.*

In Pennsylvania, where the children were not allowed their playthings on Sunday, whirligigs were called Sabbath Day toys. With his militaristic pomposity, the Hessian soldier is a perfect subject for the whirligig. *Circa* 1800. Painted wood, height 36¾″. *Herbert W. Hemphill, Jr.*

46

the vocabulary of folk art is so disparate. It doesn't have any easy sort of classification.

SF You can't make easy attributions.

MH Right. You can't say that a certain piece worked into such and such a ritual and was probably by such and such a carver from such and such a period and is the third best one known.

SF Nice museum criteria.

MH Nice, close, curatorial, compact categorizations. Right? What can I say? You're not going to be able to do that with folk art and especially not in this show.

SF No, that's right. There's a tremendous range.

MH And that's what's so marvelously American about it. Now I can wax a little chauvinistic, I guess. Diversity is one part of our identity. If the melting pot theory has any substance at all, it should be absolutely manifest in our folk art production. In my opinion, it is. And if our political value or our collective national psyche has a character, it might have to do with a spirit that is really independent, frontier, inventive, ingenious—all those clichés out of the high school history books. Why shouldn't we find it in our indigenous production? In my opinion, we do. But having found it, we have difficulty living with it. It would be easier if it all looked alike and if it all grew out of a common value, a common vision. If we could box it all up and package it, we'd have it made. But we can't, though others think we can. We're in a fight about it a lot, and we've only started to fight. I'm one of the fighters. I really love this argument. And more people are getting into the act. Some of them, in my opinion, not particularly qualified, but I suppose everybody should take their shot.

I think you begin with an exploration of the kind of material in this show. Curatorially, I suppose, we're still talking about a handful of things. If you get the right handful, you've got the picture. All the lesser things fall out, fall in line somewhere behind. The show is only as good as the best things we can assemble. Not to be able to borrow three or four of the critical pieces is to amputate an arm. That's very funny, when those things finally matter, they matter that much. When they don't, then it's something of another order. It's like dealing with the Renaissance. To not deal with . . .

SF . . . The monuments and the masterworks, yes.

MH The Sistine Chapel. And even within that, to not deal with the Last Judgment fresco. To miss these things is to miss that ringing, soaring statement that confirms and validates a time, a view, a history, and, therefore, us. That's important to me. I like the idea of the show. I like what I think is being lent. I like what I think you people

Propellers on The Sport World whirligig-vane, which was made near Gap, Pennsylvania (*circa* 1910), move figures engaged in sports and games of the period: seesaw, a kind of rudimentary merry-go-round, and boxing (the two boxers are missing). Painted wood with iron, gesso, and composition shingles, length 90″. *Collection of Michael and Julie Hall.*

Samuel Williston, the owner of the flying eagle (1800–1820), founded the Williston Academy in East Hampton, Massachusetts, with the fortune made at his button factory. Either this eagle or the one now atop the academy flagpole was the factory's trade sign. Painted pine, height 36″. *Museum of Fine Arts, Boston, John Wheelock Elliot Fund.*

"'Old Schimmel' the German who for many years tramped through this and adjoining counties making his headquarters in jails and almshouses, died at the almshouse on Sunday. His only occupation was carving heads of animals out of soft pine wood. These he would sell for a few pennies each. He was apparently a man of very surly disposition" (Carlisle, Pennsylvania *Evening Sentinel*, August 7, 1890). This eagle is a singular example of Wilhelm Schimmel's work. It is the only one known with a United States seal and is a delightful tribute to both his homeland, with its suggestion of the Hapsburgian eagle, and to his adopted country. Pennsylvania, *circa* 1870–90. Painted pine, height 10¼″. *Mr. and Mrs. James O. Keene.*

Very few documented examples of 18th-century decoys are extant. The red-breasted merganser drake decoy, made by T. Williams in 1790, is one of three known to have survived from the same hunter's rig. The others are in the collections of Adele Earnest and The Museums at Stony Brook. Long Island, New York. Painted wood with root head, length 16¼″. *Herbert W. Hemphill, Jr.*

have gone after and I miss everything that mattered and didn't come. We're going to have to live with that. But if the critics and the public can deal with the show as a significant 60 percent of the material, I can live with that. It may still work.

"American Folk Sculpture: The Personal and the Eccentric" [Cranbrook Academy of Arts Gallery, 1971] was organized at a time when folk art was easier to borrow. Bert Hemphill and I just sat down and made a list. It was one of those great games you play in your mind late at night. The Super Show. If we could put together sixty items, what would they be? With no consideration of what was or wasn't available, no consideration of size, scale, rarity, value—any of that. We just listed sixty items, and we got forty of them. It was marvelous, but it won't happen again.

SF It's like every other thing.

MH Sure. These things are national treasures now. But in those days, they were curiosities. It wasn't really that long ago, but people were interested in them as a new thing. Now they realize that everyone is competing for them. In the Bicentennial period, everybody is trying to corner the market. I still don't think folk art is understood very well. It's still abused and looked on as curious—a lesser interpretation. It doesn't matter. It's been hard, and I really think you people are to be congratulated on the quality of what you've been able to put together. The show is *about* something. I hope it's understood and that it starts the conversation.

SF Yes, that's what I hope too. That people will penetrate through to the serious level of the objects and not see them just as charming or quaint.

MH I'm death on that. I've never seen them that way. If that's what they were to me, I wouldn't collect.

SF You never even went through that stage?

MH Never. And I don't know why. It seems like such an easy place to start.

SF You first saw folk art in Kentucky?

MH I first saw it right here in New York—by accident—ten years ago at the Museum of American Folk Art. I was on my way to the Modern and had fifteen minutes to kill. My wife, Julie, and I just walked up the stairs and fell into a great show called "Collector's Choice, Part One." Bert had curated the show, and it was some of the very important things brought together from collections in the area. I guess you call them "filler" shows in the business—the great things that some curator feels should be brought together one more time. Wham! It just came out of the sky. Knocked Julie and me out—for reasons that I can't really explain, except that we were

open to it that day. It spoke and we listened. And the more we listened, the more we could comprehend. It started like that; it was dramatic. Revelation is sometimes very slow and then sometimes very intense. This was intense, and we came into it right away. That was the appeal. We saw something at work, something we really didn't know about in any historical sense. That was the whole interaction between Bert and us: he had the history, we had the outside objectivity. We were outsiders, artists.

SF Fresh to the whole thing.

MH Fresh off the street! We'd never heard of New England family portraits or John Brewster and had never heard of Wilhelm Schimmel. And didn't need to at that point. It was so electric. Bert fascinated us—the insight that he had and the experience that he had with the material. We fascinated him for the naive enthusiasm that is a kind of privileged insight. Up until that time, I guess he had never run into anyone who was able to come to folk art so freely, who didn't have an easy introduction, who hadn't been brought up with it or turned on to it through an antique shop orientation, who didn't see it as a complement for painted furniture or what have you.

It was really that stark. We knew about African things and about Oceanic things, pre-Columbian things, modern things, but this was brand new. And it was loud and clear; and it's been loud and clear ever since. What we saw then and what we're seeing now hasn't changed that much. Our understanding of what we're seeing now has been complemented by the history and experience that we've built through seeing more collections and reading more books. They've given us a familiarity with folk art as a collecting area, as a body of things. Our understanding helps us determine that very tight selection, where this matters and that might matter and that doesn't seem to matter much at all. We draw those lines; we still make those late night lists.

SF That's a wonderful collector's game.

MH It is *the* collector's game.

SF The collection without walls.

MH It exists as an ideal and it presupposes criteria. The criteria tighten and focus within a panorama that's always expanding because new items come to light, because you see something that you didn't know existed. Something you have to find a place for. You have to bring it into the embrace. So you get an expanding overview, and yet you get a narrowing or focusing insight that has to deal with more material all the time. Collecting becomes structured that way. It becomes intense

49

This carving of Buffalo Bill Cody is from a group of about forty genre tableaux of the panorama of American life that were displayed together in a Vermont country store. Though made in Vermont *circa* 1910, they show a marked French Canadian influence. Cherry and maple wood with leather trim and ivory buttons, height 18". *The Margaret Woodbury Strong Museum.*

that way. It's better now than it was in the beginning. We started out looking at a handful of things and we've now seen thousands of items and owned hundreds. Some stay and some don't.

A perfect example of one of the causes of a typical collector's mania is Brooklyn's *Bicycle Rider*. I'm mad for it. I would own it in a minute. But that thing was under all our noses, you know. The first time I saw it, I knew that you already had it. What can I say? You were right to move on it quickly. That's collecting, right? Everybody's got those stories—the one that got away. Then there are the other stories, the ones that you landed. Crazy, curious conjunction of timing and circumstances and preparation, and—boom!—it's yours. The *Newsboy* is one we landed.

SF That's very recent, isn't it?

MH Within the last eight months. It just came to us. If we didn't believe that something as fantastic as that is still out there somewhere and that we could tie into it as easily as the next guy, it would be terribly depressing. That's the thing that keeps dealers alive and collectors hungry. It's almost unbelievable. Forty-five or fifty years of intense collecting, combing the barns and the attics and the basements, third generation collectors,

and yet, something like that just appears. And it's right. You know it's right from head to toe. An untouched figure of that much beauty, that much power, that much expression, that much scale.

It's crazy, you know. Every collection is built a piece at a time. I think the public never fully understands that. I think museums sometimes don't understand it. Ninety percent of the time, I don't believe that a curator really knows what he asks for when he asks for a loan. I'm sorry, but I think that's true. I also think that museums sometimes don't understand their own collections, for even a museum collection is built a piece at a time. If it's a gift, it means that it went through all the birth agony with a private collector who then donated it. Or a curator takes a position and starts to build, and then his role changes or he moves to another institution and someone inherits the legacy and looks on it as just "stuff." We forget that it was pulled out of the woodwork, a piece at a time. Every piece in every collection has always got a story, sometimes of that backdoor where you slid into the thing sideways and—lo and behold— it was yours. All you did was pick it up and write a check. Sometimes there are furious scrambles and intrigue and acing out. We've done it all.

Man with Grapes,
Wells, Maine,
circa 1850.
Painted wood with
ivory eyes,
height 15½″. *Private
Collection.*

Doll, first quarter of the
19th century. Wood,
height 6″. *Private
Collection.*

The collectors are mad. I love all my mad collectors. I love them for their madness. I can't account for it, but a collector starts to form a taste and starts to have the means to collect: contacts, of course, and financial resources, which may be a factor . . . may not. I'm a schoolteacher, but I scramble hard. That has a lot to do with it. There are ways to offset liabilities or deficiencies.

I think almost anyone can collect. All you have to do is have the disease, the rest will take care of itself. There will be the furious years when the learning pieces are bought, to be sold later. Then there will be very tight years when the collection becomes a statement. If it's a valid collection, it is a statement in its own right. It's constantly creative. It is a declaration of self. I will own this, I won't own that. And the sum total of the parts becoming the whole is finally the man, finally the collector, the collection. That's one of the great things about our collection, because we have two very complementary tastes involved.

SF Perceiving, collecting, and doing it together.

MH Yes, we do it together, but we don't have the same tastes. It's not a his-and-hers kind of thing. It's electric. She's great, you know. She straightens me out and vice

versa. So we really have a double overview that embraces a wider range of things and yet synthesizes into a collective unit, the body corporate, the whole thing.

SF It doesn't come to an end, does it. It never comes to the point where you say, "Well, I've had enough now. I'll stop."

MH No, historically, that doesn't seem to be true. We find that collections close. The collection starts to be selective, and you have those things that are the core, that *are* the collection, and then the collection closes— which doesn't mean that a piece or two isn't added here and there. But as a statement, it is done. Dealers are very aware of this—too aware, in fact. They always seem to be looking for the collection that is starting to close, because that's where the action is. The collection comes together and then sometimes it's discarded and goes to auction. It's split up again and the fragments then filter out and fall into a new orientation: their conjunction with other things in other hands. I think it's very healthy; I don't have any problems with it. Sometimes, of course, the collection goes, in toto, to a sponsoring institution like a museum. That's reasonable too. Providing, of course, the care and the love are still there. Nothing is sadder than an unloved collection.

51

This figure from South Carolina may be Eve, but the woman's relationship with the snake suggests a connection with the snake cults that still exist in remote sections of the South. *Circa* 1920. Wood, height 40". *The Marvill Collection.*

SF Yes, better for it to be in the hands of people who can care for it than to be tucked away and neglected.

MH Witness the recent dispersion of the Mackey decoy collection. *The* great collection and now it's a part of the life of hundreds of other collections. It starts again. I think of it as an ecological kind of thing. It's a wonderful system that sustains itself and is very important. I can't overestimate the value of private collectors. Of course, it's terribly important to us, but I mean all the way around, too.

SF Your pieces in the show were among the first that I saw and one of the reasons for my instant excitement with the show. Are any of your earliest acquisitions in this show, or are they mostly later things?

MH The show is really a pretty good cross section of the whole period of our collecting. The *Man with the Pony* came to us in the first year. The *Sport World* came to us within the first year and a half. The *Miss Liberty* figure within the first two years. In fact, we had very good luck.

SF You certainly did.

MH We found some of the great things when not a lot of people were looking at this particular vocabulary. I can't explain it. Certainly, the conventional material—the factory weather vanes and the cigar store Indians—had been avidly collected for years. But the more personal, one-of-a-kind, eccentric area was still wide open. Some of the earlier collectors had understood it and had shown appreciation for it. But it was still rather catch-as-catch-can. If you had a feeling for it, it came in as a complement to mainstream or mainline—what can I call it?—blue chip material. *The Index of American Design* type of work. A lot of what we're looking at and a lot of what is in this exhibition certainly never would have made it into the *Index.* For the most part, it was still anathema to the collecting community in the mid-60's. It didn't mean much even here in New York until '70 or '71, when a new group of dealers and a new group of collectors, inspired with a new value, a whole new cultural review, started to find it significant and started to listen to the kind of arguments that I've offered here. They started to look at a wider range of things and suddenly discovered a treasure trove. It had been here all along but had been overlooked because it seemed odd or shoddy or not credible because it was without precedent. It was a little too offbeat. I think very few people looked at this material besides collectors like Bert Hemphill and Adele Earnest, who have the kind of eye that has always responded to these things. But it takes a collective commitment to make it a visible collecting area, to make it the kind of thing a museum is interested in or the kind of thing that the general public or the art community or the critical

52

community will make a space for. It takes even more to assert that this new material might even displace some of the traditional material and replace the traditional values and criteria of what it is we want American folk art to be.

In the late 60's there were only a handful of people competing for this material. There are hundreds of people looking for it now.

SF   In that short space of time?

MH   Yes, in that short space of time. It wasn't even profitable for dealers then. It's very profitable now and that always creates a climate of speculation. It also produces second and third waves of collectors who get involved in it for reasons that may not be as personal as the vision that moved the first wave.

SF   The followers.

MH   Yes, following a taste. Then, of course, you get that inevitable barrage of things that look like what you're talking about but may not be. If an *Index* horse is a standard of one taste, then other things that seem to resemble it have a place and have a value and move into the collectible area. If something like the *Bicycle Rider* comes down, it's going to move into a challenging position, and then the *Bicycle Rider* itself becomes the standard. It stands or falls as it faces new challengers. I think

that's good, because it helps form a collective judgment. Certainly there are visionary people among us who can make a statement or take a position, but they cannot dictate.

SF   It's a sifting process.

MH   It's sifting and sorting, evaluating and comparing. The thrill is that it's not a static system. Tolson's work rose up as a challenge, which still hasn't been settled. A lot of people still have big reservations about it. They think Tolson's a simple country craftsman whose statement is very limited, whose images are repetitive, whose skills are only manual. Based on their inspection of the material, he's only the best of the mountain whittlers.

The *Bicycle Rider* pops up. One of the great surreal, brutal, singular images—a trade store piece. All of a sudden a lot of other rude, crude things are offered as the same thing. Are they the same thing? Put them next to the *Bicycle Rider* and you'll find out. You'll find out in two-and-a-half seconds. I know the *Bicycle Rider* will stand. I knew it the day I saw it. And I'm not possessed of any great powers of divination. It's just that good to me. And that definitional. That's what a collector looks for.

The *Newsboy* will stand. The Ohio black figures will stand. The *Man with the Pony* will stand. And we're humble to live with those things. It's a real experience.

Preacher, found in North Carolina, early 20th century. Painted wood, height 10″. *Mr. and Mrs. Roderick Moore.*

53

American Folk Sculpture: Some considerations of its ethnic heritage

by Michael Kan
*Curator of African, Oceanic,
and New World Cultures
The Brooklyn Museum*

The full story of American folk sculpture cannot be accurately told without some discussion of its ethnic heritage, of the traditions that lie outside the Anglo-American mainstream but interlock with it in ever varying patterns. Since this essay is limited in scope, it is impossible to deal here with all the ethnic traditions that have contributed to the development of American folk sculpture. Only the Afro-American and the Spanish-American traditions (specifically the *santos* tradition of New Mexico) will be discussed. The two are vastly different for a variety of historical and cultural reasons.

African slaves were brought to this country with their families and culture all but shattered. On the other hand, the carvers of *santos* in the southwestern United States brought with them the full spectrum of their New World–Spanish traditions. The African slaves were forced to adapt to an Anglo-American way of life, whereas the New Mexicans lived in isolation, away from both their mother culture and that of the Anglo-American. It is this isolation that caused their culture and art to develop a quality unique unto itself. Afro-American culture, from the earliest period on, tended to be more of a hybrid. Survivals, by and large, consist of aesthetic patterns, often of a conceptual nature, which are frequently hard to pinpoint without documentation.

The kinds of questions left unanswered because of the lack of specific documentation become apparent in a discussion of the magnificent pair of black men, all decked out in their Sunday best, from the Michael and Julie Hall collection. How is one to know with certainty, in the absence of data, whether the carver was black or white? Still, there is something about the sensitive handling of the head and features, in marked contrast to the more generalized handling of the body, that recalls a characteristic frequently found in the traditional art of Africa. The visual evidence at hand suggests that the carver of *Two Black Figures* was not trying to caricature the Afro-American, but was trying to bring out a nobility in their presence. One can easily approach these sculptures with the same system used by Robert Farris Thompson to identify the hand which carved the well-known seated male figure holding a small bucket from Fayetteville, New York (Abby Aldrich Rockefeller Folk Art Collection). He writes:

> The attribution is based on the fact that no trace of caricature or social distance, between maker and subject, can be

These two black figures (*circa* 1880) may have been used in funeral rites in a lodge or church. The left figure surely held a Bible; the one on the right has a loop in his lapel for a fresh flower. Hamilton, Ohio. Wood and mixed media, height 56½″ and 53¾″. *Collection of Michael and Julie Hall.*

55

detected. This is extremely rare for a century when the Afro-American as grotesque was all the rage in the lithographs of Currier and Ives and black-faced performers in minstrelsy parodied a world they never understood. The manly dignity of the image at hand is removed from the half-apologetic, half-ingratiating smiles of this other world. If the piece was carved by an Anglo-American, his sympathy for his subject and the cultural accuracy of his stylistic means were amazing for his century and would almost make him qualify as a kind of honorary Afro-American in the manner of John Brown.[1]

The lack of documentation is just one of the problems facing the scholar in the study of American folk sculpture. I hope in this essay to clarify certain gray areas, and to point the way to further avenues of fruitful scholarship.

Even by the early 1960's it was still generally held that African institutions had not survived the traumatic cultural upheaval of North American slavery, and as a result, African influences on American art had been negligible, except for a few survivals in the fields of music, dance, and folklore. Typifying this point of view was the position taken by Charles E. Silberman in his book *Crisis in Black and White*, where he suggests that the African slave, unlike other immigrant people, brought little of their rich cultural heritage to America.[2] An early dissenting voice was that of James A. Porter who, in *Modern Negro Art*, first brought attention to the unique role of the slave artist and craftsman in the arts and decorative arts of North America.[3] In a later work, he raises the question of African survivals in the "peculiarities of surface design" that were noted on some unusual stoneware effigy vessels made by Afro-Americans in South Carolina.[4]

In 1969 Robert Farris Thompson published "African Influences on the Art of the United States," a thesis which has forced the scholarly world to rethink the whole problem of Sub Saharan Africa's contribution to American art history. In it he writes:

> The suppression of the more public African influences, such as religious ritual and the use of subsaharan costume, did not still the voice of more intimate expressions. Present to this day are African-influenced verbal arts (Aunt Nancy tales), healing (conjuring), cuisine (hog maws and collard greens), singing (field hollers and work songs), and dance forms in considerable quantity. And present, too, are parallel visual continuities: amazing stoneware vessels shaped in the form of anguished human faces made by Afro-Americans in South Carolina in the last century, multiple wood carving modes in tidewater Georgia, basketry modes of astonishing purity near Charleston, the deliberate decoration of graves in the African manner with surface deposits of broken earthenware and possessions in many parts of the Deep South, and isolated instances of Afro-American wood carving in Livingston County, Missouri,

and Onondaga County, New York. If these visual traditions are less blatant than the programs of costuming, sculpture, and the dance with which Afro-Cubans used to bring their street fiestas to proper aesthetic pitch, they are no less valid for this difference. By the hand of individual Afro-American masters were fashioned works of art whose blending of remembered ancestral and encountered alien modes may now be estimated and explored.[5]

Effigy Vessels of South Carolina

There are numerous documented examples in North America of African technological survivals related to the making of tools, utensils, and even musical instruments. Many of the slaves brought with them a variety of craft skills from ironworking to weaving.

A variety of stoneware effigy vessels were covered with an olive-gray ash glaze characteristic of many South Carolina potteries. *Effigy Jug* and *Face Jug* were thrown on a simple kick-wheel and roughly resemble the bottom part of a jug without handle or spout. The features were hand-modeled onto the wheel-thrown form, turning it into a grotesque head, snarling with an almost demoniac ferocity. Fillets of modeled clay were probably used to fashion the ears and eyebrows that arch downward to form the high bridge of the nose. An open, protruding mouth reveals a set of clenched teeth that were fashioned with a sharp stick or similar instrument and are usually treated with a high firing white china clay (kaolin). The same white china clay is used on the protruding eyeballs set in rounded sockets.

These highly distinctive effigy vessels have been uncritically referred to as "monkey jugs," "slave jugs," "water jugs," and even "voodoo pots." However, Thompson has coined the more accurate term "Afro-Carolinian face vessels,"[6] a term which makes us appreciate the identity of their makers as well as the locale of their manufacture.

It appears that the Civil War created an extra demand for stoneware, which was met in 1863 by the pottery on the plantation of Colonel Thomas J. Davis of Bath in Aiken County, South Carolina. Since labor was scarce, a great many Afro-American craftsmen, recruited from the slave ranks, were put to work in the pottery. Soon, through their own initiative, these craftsmen were fashioning small effigy face vessels for their own use. The tradition lasted for a short, two-year period, for General Sherman set fire to the Davis pottery in 1865.[7]

The hybridization which occurs when Afro-American craftsmen work pottery in what is essentially an Anglo-American technique is typical of the problem encountered by the scholar investigating African survivals in

Effigy Jug, Bath, South Carolina, *circa* 1817. Glazed clay, height 7½". *Augusta-Richmond County Museum.*

Although face jugs are functional items, this one from Montgomery County, Pennsylvania, was probably not made for use. *Circa* 1805. Stoneware with salt glaze and blue cobalt decoration, height 8". *Private Collection.*

Head. Africa, Sierra Leone, Sherbro Island, Bullom or Sherbro. Steatite, height 10¼". *Courtesy of The Museum of Primitive Art, New York.* Nail Fetish Figure (detail). Africa, Zaïre, Kongo. Wood, pigment, metal, and glass, height 33⅞". *The Brooklyn Museum.*

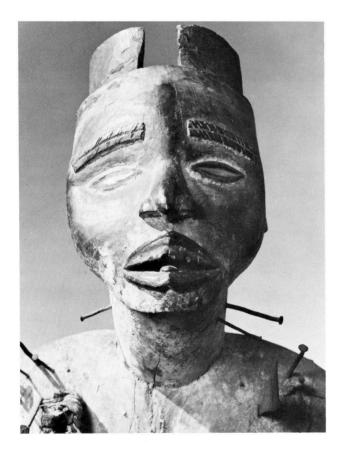

American folk sculpture. What can we focus upon specifically in this tradition which owes its inspiration to Africa? The wheel-thrown jug-like form is typically European. The concept of making effigy vessels in the form of human heads had both African and European precedents. In fact, *Face Jug,* which is from Montgomery County, Pennsylvania (*circa* 1805), superficially resembles the Afro-Carolinian example. The traditional English toby jug is still another possible prototype, yet as Thompson points out, "The Aiken County masters created a face in a manner light years removed from the courtly toby jug."[8]

Turning to possible African sources of inspiration, Judith W. Chase suggests that familiar African forms could have been transferred from one material to another. She makes the somewhat simplistic suggestion that the Aiken County vessels could have been derived from Pende effigy wooden cups from Zaïre[9]—a superficial comparison which is supported only on visual grounds and without other evidence.

The concept of African forms being transferred from one material in Africa to another in America is not in itself farfetched. However, a much stronger case can be made for the Sherbro soapstone human heads from Sierra Leone as possible antecedents to the Afro-Carolinian vessels. Both share the enormous protruding eyes and the large open mouth full of clenched teeth. Furthermore, it has been firmly established that, in the eighteenth and early nineteenth centuries, a great many slaves were brought to South Carolina from the Gambia-Sierra Leone area, exceeded only in numbers by those from the Lower Congo and Angola.[10]

It has been pointed out that one of the most distinctive and unique features of the Aiken County effigy vessels is the way in which white china clay was used to inset eyes and teeth. Thompson has made the fascinating observation that this feature has no European precedents, but seems to relate closely in its aesthetic to Kongo figural carving in wood.[11] A detail from a typical nail fetish from this area reveals an extraordinary affinity with the Afro-Carolinian vessel style. The eyes with pupils pinpointed with embedded glass correspond to the whitened kaolin eyes. Also shared are the open mouth with clenched teeth and the high-bridged nose.

What function could these Aiken County effigy vessels have served? Did they act as charms or funerary vessels, or simply as status objects? Without further documentation, these questions may never be answered. We can be sure, however, that these masterful expressionistic pieces were made by people of African descent for their own use and not for Anglo-American consumption.

New Orleans and Voodoo

Baron Samedi, a large, dramatic, puppet-like figure, has been discussed by Robert Bishop in his book, *American Folk Sculpture.*

> The practice of voodoo originated in Africa and was transported to America by slaves. The voodoo religion is characterized by a belief in sorcery, fetishes, and rituals in which participants communicate by trance with ancestors, saints, or animalistic deities. Carved figures are believed to increase the potency of the fetish, spell, or curse. This figure was found covered with blood and chicken feathers in a black barbershop in New Orleans. Special shops servicing practitioners of this black-magic religion continue to exist in cities like New York, Philadelphia, and New Orleans.[12]

Attributions such as this are hard to establish on the basis of the scant body of literature concerning voodoo as practiced in New Orleans. Without reliable firsthand documentation of actual practices and ceremonies, it is almost impossible to establish iconographic distinctions among the complex array of supernatural beings known as *loas*.

What is the basis for the attribution of *Baron Samedi?* First, it was found covered with sacrificial material (blood and chicken feathers) associated with voodoo ritual; and second, the interlocked figure eight designs running up and down his tin chest can be interpreted as representing its skeletal structure, which would imply an association with death.[13]

Some of the complexity of *loa* iconography can be gleaned from this analysis by Janheinz Jahn.

> The loas of the *Guédé* group are gods of death; grotesque, absurd figures mostly, and very obscene. The most important among them is *Baron Samedi* or *Baron cimitière* or *Baron-la-Croix* or *Maître-Cimetière-Boumba*. On his black altar stands a black wooden cross ornamented with silver. It is the same one that, in connection with Legba, symbolizes life, for the kingdom of the invisible ones, of the life forces, is at the same time the cosmic graveyard, into which those who have died enter, and sink into the depth of the waters to rise again as loas. Thus the cross of the meeting of the visible with the invisible symbolizes at the same time the unity of life and death. Every Voodoo ceremony, therefore, begins with the invocation of Legba and closes with the salutation to the god of the dead Guédé. The dancer whom Guédé mounts lets himself fall to the ground, holds his breath, and does not move again. Other loas of the Guédé group are symbolized by pickaxe, shovel, skull, crossbones or withered leaves—indicating clearly their functions in connection with death.[14]

Another possibility that cannot be overlooked is that the articulated limbs of *Baron Samedi* might have been designed to accommodate clothing. If this is the case, the figure could originally have had a very different appearance. The designs down his chest, presently interpreted as a representation of a skeletal system, might then be

59

Baron Samedi (*circa* 1930) was found during the course of restoration in the backroom of what had been a barbershop in the Vieux Carre in New Orleans. Painted wood and metal, height 32¾". *Herbert W. Hemphill, Jr.*

equated with braid on a military costume. This, in turn, would make the figure a likely candidate to assume the identity of a *loa* of the Ogou group, many of which appear in military costume. This is because *loas* in this category are derived from Ogun (Gun in Dahomey), the Yoruba deity of heat, fire, iron, and war. The two most important are Ogou Ferraille, the deity of blacksmiths, and Ogou Badagri, the warrior *loa*. Both appear in military apparel and frequently brandish great knives.[15]

Afro-American Staffs and Walking Sticks

Staffs (used as a generic term to include such things as batons and canes) were clearly an important prestige item in traditional West African cultures. They were frequently embellished with images embodying a rich iconography. The embellishing symbols generally reinforced the formal or informal status of their bearers.[16] A good example is the linguist staff of the Akan people in Ghana and Ivory Coast. Linguists were selected from a class of elders to act as spokesmen for Akan chiefs. Their elaborate staffs, with a symbolic emblem affixed to the top, were formal symbols of office. The emblem suggested either proverbs, historical incidents, or qualities that the ruler should possess.[17]

There is good evidence that this African tradition of staffs embellished with symbols, or at least some part of this tradition, survived in Afro-American art. Perhaps the best documented and most widely known example is the walking stick carved by the Afro-American blacksmith, Henry Gudgell, who lived in Livingston County, Missouri.

Gudgell was born in the early nineteenth century into a slave family in Kentucky, a state which had a history of slave immigration from southern coastal states. Like his famous Northwest Indian counterpart, Charles Edenshaw, he appears to have been a brilliant craftman in many fields, excelling not only in his specialized fields of smithing and wheelwrighting, but also as a woodcarver, silversmith, and coppersmith.

The walking stick was carved for John Bryan, a close friend of Gudgell's master, who was wounded in the Civil War and limped for the rest of his life. It remained in the Bryan family until 1968, when it was sold to the Yale University Art Gallery.[18] This unique documented work was carved out of a sturdy light-colored wood. Like so many West African carvings, the wood was originally stained a deep black. Most of the dark color has been worn off the areas that were carved in highest relief.

From bottom to top, the following representations are shown along the shaft. A snake entwines itself around the lower register of the cane as if it were on a tree trunk. Further up, a fully dressed human figure clutches the shaft with hands and flexed legs, as though trying to escape by climbing away from the serpent. This interpretation seems to be reinforced by a forked branch sprouting leaves that opposes the human figure on the other side of the shaft. Continuing up the stick, in sequence, carved as though seen from above, one finds a beautifully conceived tortoise and a lizard. How curious that this is the very same combination of animals that one typically finds on Yoruba carvings such as the Shango container presently in the Merton Simpson collection. Indeed, these animals, both singly and in combination, are found with great frequency in the art of West Africa.

Further examination of the seemingly unrelated images carved on the Gudgell walking stick hauntingly recalls the Woyo pot lids of the Lower Congo, which A.A. Gerbrands cites as classic examples of the African proverb as "image-symbol." The African knows the proverb both as "word-symbol" and "image-symbol." The two concepts are so closely related that one cannot understand the representational significance of the object without knowing the proverb.[19] For instance, if we study a Woyo pot lid in The Brooklyn Museum collection, we see that it is decorated with a figure of a man in the center, carved in-the-round. His legs are drawn up under his chin, with arms folded over his knees. Behind him, in high relief, lies a woman on a mat holding her stomach. Beside him are two other objects.

The meaning of this composition would be impossible to fathom were it not for some information gathered by the Fathers Vissers, relating to the pot lids collected by them in Woyo territory. Based on a similar pot lid, illustrated in plate 15, figure 2 of Gerbrand's article, the significance of the Brooklyn pot lid can be reconstructed as follows: "*Significance*: the man is sitting with his back to his wife, who is lying on the sleeping-mat (ill or lazy) and not doing anything (there is no cooking-pot on the fire). He complains that he had to give expensive bride-presents to her family for her (the three flasks of gin), and ends, with a sigh, that he had better take a new pipe, i.e., take a new wife."[20]

Woyo pot lids represent just one of the better documented examples of the use of stories or proverbs as image-symbols in West African sculpture, but it is clearly a strong and widely distributed tradition. Surely this tradition must have survived in more than one form in the Afro-American sculpture of the New World. More concentrated research along these lines should prove most rewarding.

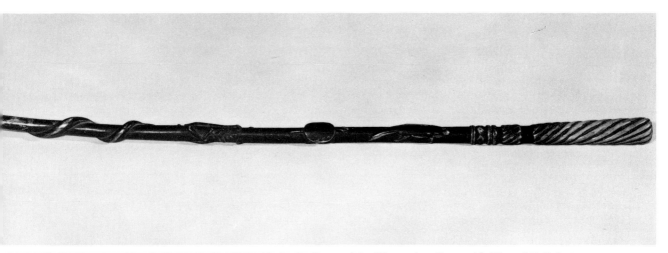

Afro-Missourian Cane with Figural Relief, *circa* 1863. Henry Gudgell (1826-95). Wood, height 36¼″. *Yale University Art Gallery.*

Container for Shango Altar. Africa, Nigeria, Yoruba. Wood, height 13½″. *Merton D. Simpson Collection, New York.*

Pot Lid. Africa, Zaïre, Woyo. Wood, diameter 8″. *The Brooklyn Museum.*

61

Carved walking sticks in the Afro-American vein occur in other areas of the United States, notably from the state of Georgia. Here again, as in Missouri, the canes are embellished with figures in high relief. Snakes, lizards, tortoises, and frogs seem to be favored as subject matter, just as they are in West Africa.[21]

One particular theme, "the snake about to swallow a frog" (or, for that matter, a mouse or some other small animal), appears with some frequency either as a relief carving on a walking stick, or, in an even more imaginative version, *Snake Swallowing a Frog*, the crooked stick itself is used to suggest the serpentine body. One recalls that the same animals (snake, tortoise, and lizard) on the Gudgell walking stick were also found associated with the Yoruba container. Along the same lines, we find the "snake swallowing a frog" theme depicted in a magnificent cast gold ornament made by the Ebrié people of Ivory Coast. In this example, however, the snake is tightly coiled, having seized its prey.

The Afro-American preference for reptilian representations in their carvings can be seen also in the work of James Cooper of Port Wentworth near Savannah, Georgia. Cooper's ability as a carver of walking sticks was implicit in his nickname, "Stick Daddy" (a close parallel to the African custom of giving a man a "praise name" based on his outstanding achievements). His favorite motifs, we are told, were snakes, tortoises, and alligators, which, like their African prototypes, were shown flattened, as if seen from above.[22]

Snake Swallowing a Frog, Georgia, 19th century. Painted wood, height 31". *Karen Sebiri.*

Pendant in form of a Snake. Africa, Ivory Coast, Ebrié, *circa* 1800. Gold, diameter 3⁹⁄₁₆". *The Brooklyn Museum, Frank L. Babbott Fund.*

Left: Snake Cane, 19th century. Painted wood, height 35¼″. *Private Collection.*

Right: This serpentine cane, said to be made for John Philippe, an Indian trader, early in the 19th century, is similar to ones made by the Sioux Indians. The twisted vine suggests a snake circling around a staff. Detroit, Michigan. Grape vine, length 34½″.
Mr. and Mrs. James O. Keene.

Snake Trivet, *circa* 1800. Iron, diameter 4″.
Mr. and Mrs. Harvey Kahn.

Fred Blair (*circa* 1901-73) was a farmer and printer in Woodbury, Tennessee, who made animal sculptures during the Depression. His work included several lizards. *Circa* 1930. Painted wood, length 25″. *Private Collection.*

63

St. EOM in
front of his
ceremonial
house
compound.
Buenavista,
Georgia.

William Edmondson (*circa* 1865-1951) was a black sculptor from Nashville, Tennessee. After working at various jobs, he became an apprentice stone layer at the age of sixty. Five years later he had a vision in which God exhorted him to carve figures in stone, which he did until his death. His figures often came from a Christian context; Eve is considered his finest work. Limestone, height 32″. *Tennessee Botanical Gardens and Fine Arts Center, Gift of Mrs. Alfred Starr.*

Afro-American Folk Sculpture of the Twentieth Century

African influences in twentieth-century Afro-American folk sculpture appear for the most part to be revivals, rather than survivals, of African tradition, and are therefore beyond the scope of this essay. The study of these fascinating and complex relationships represents a highly specialized area of study.

One is struck by the complex of influences evident in the twentieth-century work of folk sculptors such as Edmondson and Saint EOM (the initials for Eddie Owens Martin). In the latter's ceremonial house compound outside Buenavista, Georgia, a group of elaborately decorated buildings, inspired for the most part by the temples of Kathmandu, Nepal (as seen in *National Geographic*), are joined by a series of modeled walls and platforms, plastered and painted like the walls of the palace of the former kings of Dahomey at Abomey. Modeled and painted on these walls are African masks and East Indian gods, juxtaposed and blended according to St. EOM's romantic and mystical vision.

In the art of St. EOM, as in the art of many twentieth-century Afro-American folk sculptors, the African influences are not specific, nor are they traceable to a particular cultural background. Forms and symbols were selected for inclusion in the St. EOM complex primarily for their visual appeal, and because they suggested to the artist, in a highly personal manner, the forces of life and death.[23]

The Santos of New Mexico

Santo is a general term in Spanish for a variety of sacred images. From the middle of the eighteenth century to the early twentieth, New Mexican *santos* were traditionally of two main types: the *retablo*, a flat image painted on wood, canvas, paper, leather, or metal, and the *bulto*, a sculpted image, generally carved out of soft wood, covered with gesso and painted with a combination of imported and locally acquired paints. It is this latter category of *santo* that relates to folk sculpture.

The Spanish-American folk sculptors who produced these extraordinary works were known as *santeros* and, during a period of roughly one hundred and fifty years, these largely itinerant artists plied their trade throughout the Sangre de Cristo Mountains in northern New Mexico and southern Colorado. *Santeros* probably owed their existence to the fact that New Mexico was the most remote outpost of New Spain. Until 1821 Spain prohibited all but her own territories to trade with this area. As a result, the people of New Mexico were forced to become more and more self-reliant in all respects to avoid a chronic shortage of all products that had to be shipped by the infrequent mule trains from Mexico.

Annexation by the United States in 1846 brought a new era to New Mexico. The people of this area, isolated for so long a time, now began to look eastward instead of south as stage coach service was opened in the mid-nineteenth century over the Santa Fe Trail. By the 1870's, Santa Fe had its first archbishop, Father John B. Lamy, and the city became a metropolitan see.[24]

Who made these *santos* and for whom? Isolation produced some strange groups in New Mexico, and one of the strangest and most fascinating was the *Penitentes*, or, to use their full title, *Los Hermanos Penitentes de la Tercera Orden de San Francisco*. E. Boyd quotes the following from an article that discusses the *Penitentes* in the Santa Fe *New Mexican* of April 11, 1952: "The Penitente brotherhood in rural New Mexico is one of the world's last remnants of the religious tradition of

By legend, San Acacio was a general of the
Roman legions who, with his troops,
converted to Christianity after having a
vision on the eve of a great battle. Later he
and all his men were crucified for refusing to
deny their new religion. New Mexican
santeros suggested the mass crucifixion by
placing the soldiers (or in some cases
symbolic weapons) in a row at the foot of the
cross. Figures of San Acacio were
particularly popular in the latter part of the
18th century, when New Mexico enjoyed
its greatest period of security and expansion.
The figure is generally shown in
contemporary military dress. 1890's. Painted
wood, height 39″. *Mr. and Mrs. Jimmy Ernst*

penitente orders in late medieval Europe. Little is generally known about the New Mexico brotherhood or its rituals, although they were popularized by travelers [of the past] century who emphasized that the Penitentes at that time held 'ceremonial Crucifixions.' "[25]

The most individual forms of *santo* sculpture, like the *Penitente* sect, relate more to the Christianity of medieval Europe than to the established Spanish religion of the eighteenth and nineteenth centuries. Having started by copying Spanish-Mexican eighteenth-century baroque prototypes, the *santos* rapidly evolved to differ as much from these norms as the *Penitentes* did in their religious practices. The *Penitentes* were still stressing penance and the anguish and sorrow of Holy Week when the rest of Europe and America had altered their religious views to conform to the more humanistic trends dating from the Renaissance.[26]

Most of the *santos* shown here date from the late nineteenth century or well into the twentieth. By this time the itinerant *santero* was greatly in demand in the areas far removed from the large towns. In addition to restoring the old religious figures in churches, the *santero* was frequently commissioned to carve patron saints for large rural families. Often he was paid in goods or livestock, living with the family until his work was accomplished.[27]

José Benito Ortega, "The Master of the Dotted Line," was one of the last of the notable *santeros* and was born in 1858. He was not particularly known for his technique and frequently used excessive coats of gesso to cover imperfections in the milled lumber which he used. As a result, his figures are often more likely to disintegrate than *santos* of a much earlier date.

One of Ortega's most imposing works is the monumental *San José* from the Denver Art Museum. Its flat, simplified form bears finely painted black dots around the eyes and brows and two red dots mark the center of each ear.[29]

The more "primitive" *santos*, which appeal to the contemporary eye, are actually of recent vintage. Although new methods and new iconography were pouring into New Mexico during the period of Ortega's peak of activity, his style changed very little and remained suited to the conservative tastes of his customers, who were scattered in remote villages throughout the hinterlands.[28]

It is possible that this figure of San José (*circa* 1890) once held a Christ Child and a flowering staff, the saint's usual attributes. One can see the characteristic bold carving, with special emphasis on facial features, of José Benito Ortega (1858–1941). Mora County, New Mexico. Gessoed and painted wood, height 49″. *Denver Art Museum.*

Two sculptures from the Taylor Museum, Colorado Springs Fine Arts Center, *Job* and *Death Cart*, are uniquely New Mexican in their iconography. The Job figure seems to represent a syncretic fusion of at least four Christ figure types. The late Gothic pose of Christ seated upon the Rock of Calvary has become mixed with Christ crowned with thorns or is confused with *Ecce Homo* and the Man of Sorrows. These, in turn, have become transformed into the figure of Job seated with his head cradled in his right hand. His many bleeding boils can be identified with the signs of Christ's Passion. The sorrows and anguish of Job has become associated in the mind of the northern New Mexican with the agony of Christ.[30]

The figure of Job is seated in a little niche made from an oil can. New Mexico, second half of the 19th century. Gessoed and painted cottonwood and tin, height 14½″. *Taylor Museum, Colorado Springs Fine Arts Center.*

The New Mexican *santeros* changed the familiar European figure of Death (seen here on a 19th-century Death Cart) by replacing its usual attribute—the scythe—with a bow and arrow, objects more closely associated with life in the Southwest. Probably Servilleta, New Mexico. Wood, gesso, and horsehair, length 58½″. *Taylor Museum, Colorado Springs Fine Arts Center.*

69

Nuestra Señora de la Luz was carved by José Dolores Lopez (1868–1938), one of the few *santeros* who continued working into the 20th century. He did not concentrate entirely on religious objects, but also made furniture, ornamental containers, and cemetery markers. Today, José Lopez's son George carries on his father's tradition. Cordova, New Mexico, 1936. Cottonwood, height 40".
Taylor Museum, Colorado Springs Fine Arts Center.

Death Carts or *Muertes* are some of the most terrifying sculptures produced for *Penitente* worship. They were drawn along in the simulated journey to Calvary during Holy Week. One can easily visualize these huge figures of death (nicknamed La Dona Sebastiana) surrounded by men in the procession flogging themselves with cat-o'-nine-tails or staggering along under the weight of large crosses. This is the dance of death come alive again following the great plagues of medieval Europe.

When the *Penitentes* worshiped in churches about one hundred years ago, it was their custom to keep human skulls as part of their religious paraphernalia. When they were expelled from churches and took up their worship in special religious structures, known as *moradas*, they took the skulls with them, but soon appear to have abandoned the use of actual human skulls and substituted the *Muertes*.[31]

Santeros have survived up to the present day. At least three members of the illustrious Lopez family of Cordoba remain active in a family which has produced carvers for over six generations. José Dolores Lopez developed a new style, which can be seen in *Nuestra Señora de la Luz*, which broke with the age-old traditions of the *santero* art. In lieu of polychrome painting over gesso, Lopez allows the stark white wood to show, but covers the whole surface with a lacy network of incised designs derived from filigree jewelry. He is also fond of carving elaborate biblical themes such as the Flight into Egypt and Adam and Eve, all in his distinctive, ornate style that recalls the ornamental tin work from Mexico.[32]

A discussion of these few aspects of the ethnic background of American folk sculpture reveals an untapped wealth of material waiting to be studied. The impact of two traditions, separated by vast distances in space and time, has been dealt with here. Both brought a unique flavor and idiom to these works: the Afro-American tradition through a process of hybridization with Anglo-American culture; the *santero* tradition through the retention of conservative elements that brought about a dramatic fusion of medieval religious beliefs with ideas of the twentieth-century.

1 Robert Farris Thompson, "African Influence on the Art of the United States," in *Black Studies in the University*, ed. A. L. Robinson, C. C. Foster, D. H. Olgilvie (New Haven: Yale University Press, 1969), p. 155. Cited as Thompson, 1969.

2 Charles E. Silberman, *Crisis in Black and White* (New York: Vintage Book Edition, 1964), p. 109.

3 James A. Porter, *Modern Negro Art* (New York: Dryden Press, 1943).

4 Los Angeles, California, UCLA Art Galleries, *The Negro in American Art*, 1966, "One Hundred Years of Afro-American Art" by James A. Porter, p. 6.

5 Thompson, 1969, pp. 126–27.

6 Thompson, 1969, p. 136.

7 Thompson, 1969, p. 132.

8 Thompson, 1969, p. 138.

9 Judith W. Chase, *Afro-American Art and Craft* (New York: Van Nostrand Reinhold Co., 1971), p. 57.

10 Thompson, 1969, p. 140.

11 Thompson, 1969, pp. 138–39.

12 Robert Bishop, *American Folk Sculpture* (New York: E. P. Dutton, 1974), p. 203.

13 Conversation with Herbert W. Hemphill, Jr., New York, 1975.

14 Janheinz Jahn, *Muntu: An Outline of the New African Culture* (New York: Grove Press Edition, 1961), pp. 45–46. Cited as Jahn, 1961.

15 Jahn, 1961, p. 44.

16 Conversation with Leon Siroto, New York, 1975.

17 A. A. Y. Kyerematen, *Panoply of Ghana: Ornamental Art in Ghanaian Tradition and Culture* (New York: Praeger, 1964), pp. 92–96.

18 Thompson, 1969, pp. 127–28.

19 A. A. Gerbrands, "Art as an Element of Culture Especially in Negro-Africa," *Mededelingen van het Rijksmuseum voor Volkenkunde* (Leiden) no. 12 (1956), p. 114. Cited as Gerbrands, 1957.

20 Gerbrands, 1957, p. 121.

21 Thompson, 1969, p. 145.

22 Thompson, 1969, p. 146.

23 Conversation with Lynn Kohl, New York, 1975.

24 Robert L. Shalkop, *Wooden Saints, The Santos of New Mexico* [Partial catalogue of the permanent collection of the Taylor Museum, Colorado Springs Fine Arts Center] (Feldafing: Buchheim Verlag, 1967), pp. 7–8. Cited as Shalkop, 1967.

25 E. Boyd, *Popular Arts of Spanish New Mexico* (Santa Fe: Museum of New Mexico Press, 1974), p. 457. Cited as Boyd, 1974.

26 Shalkop, 1967, p. 11.

27 Boyd, 1974, p. 407.

28 Boyd, 1974, pp. 416–25.

29 Robert Stroessner, *Santos of the Southwest* (Denver: Denver Art Museum, 1970), p. 38.

30 Shalkop, 1967, p. 44.

31 Boyd, 1974, p. 462.

32 Boyd, 1974, pp. 468–71.

72

Left: The American Flag
Gate (*circa* 1872) was
first offered in a sale of
garden furniture—it was
not deemed important
enough for an Americana
sale—but has since
become one of the most
recognized and
reproduced works of
American folk sculpture.
Changing color and light
can be seen through the
spaces between the stripes,
which are painted on both
sides. The effect is of a
flag waving on the wind—
another example of the
folk artist's ability to
solve complicated
functional, design, and
aesthetic problems.
Hudson River Valley,
New York. Painted wood
and metal, width 56″.
*Museum of American
Folk Art.*

Right: George Washington,
found in Cornwall,
Pennsylvania, 19th century.
Painted wood, height 13⅞″.
*Museum of Fine Arts,
Boston, Gift of Maxim
Karolik.*

Left: The Black Indian may date from the 18th century, which would make it one of America's earliest known whirligigs. The tradition of blending the characteristics of an American Indian with the features of a black originated with tobacco shop signs in England, where both the Blackamoor and the Noble Savage were popular exotic images. The blending also can be seen among the few figures remaining from colonial America. Painted wood, height 10″.
Mr. and Mrs. Harvey Kahn.

Right: The Schoolmaster Whirligig (*circa* 1825) holds copy slateboards with the daily exercise written on them. Painted wood, height 23½″.
Mr. and Mrs. Harvey Kahn.

Far right: Baseball Player, late 19th century. Painted and gilded wood, height 8¾″. *George Bird.*

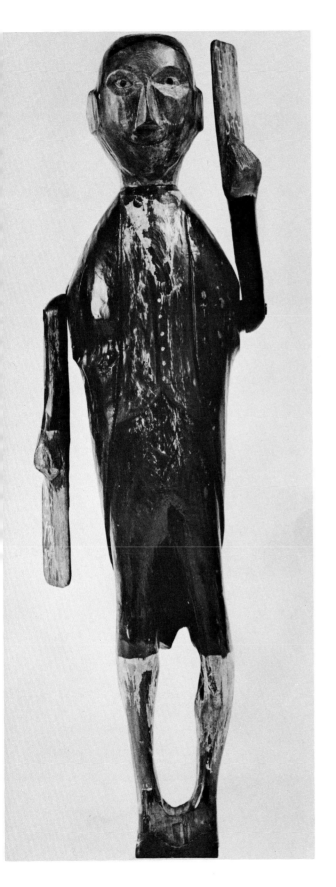

Left: Grand Turk Tavern Sign, Boston, Massachusetts, 1789. Painted wood, height 31″. *The Connecticut Historical Society*.

Below: Though the date 1776 was added during a later repainting, the sign of the Bacchus Inn in Norwich, Connecticut, can be traced at least to the 1780's. The inn itself was built well before the Revolution. This sign is similar to a sign in which the Bacchus holds grapes carved by British sailor-prisoners in 1776 in Windham, Connecticut. Painted wood, height 26½″. *The Connecticut Historical Society*.

Unlike most family knife boxes, this piece (*circa* 1875–1900) is both a functional object and a small work of sculpture. The handle is in the form of a man wearing a cap. Found in New York. Painted wood, height 15″. *The New York State Historical Association.*

Above: "1878" (Oct)" is written in pencil on the base of this figure. The dandy's costume probably reflects the fashion of the 1850's for things Scottish, a fashion inspired by Queen Victoria's family life at Balmoral. Painted wood, height 14″. *Timothy and Pamela Hill.*

79

Left: Angel, Pennsylvania, 19th century. Wood, height 8½″. *Private Collection.*

These tigers from Portland, Maine, are
attributed to Augustus Wilson, a lighthouse
keeper who was known to have "made some
tigers." Wilson lived in Portland before
moving down the coast to the Rockland area.
The carving itself suggests a practiced hand
and the painting that of a decoy maker.
There is one more tiger known from this
group. Early 20th century. Painted wood,
height 24″ and 35½″. *Private Collection.*

Right: The Reindeer Weather Vane (*circa* 1890) is typical of a style found in the Adirondacks and other mountain resort areas. It was fashionable with the visitors "roughing it" in the hotels, camps, hunting lodges, and summer cottages. Objects in this style were often made by local Indians. Wood, height 21⅝″. *Lawrence Belles.*

Below: Nanny Goat, Vermont, *circa* 1900. Painted wood, height 6¾″. *Private Collection.*

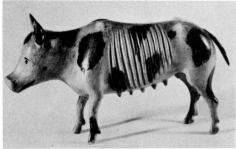

Above: The Sow (*circa* 1900) was made in Zoar, Ohio, a communal settlement known for its remarkably diverse craft and its variety of decorative styles. Painted wood, height 3¾″. *Private Collection.*

Right: Hunter's Delight, possibly Vermont, 20th century. Painted pine, height 19″. *Robert Bishop.*

81

Top left: The Touring Car (*circa* 1907) has an original
socket for turning and a weathered patina that indicates
some exposure to the elements. But there are no drain holes
in the floor, so it was probably not a weather vane.
Perhaps it was a semi-protected sign for an auto sales or
repair shop. Long Island, New York. Painted wood and
metal, length 25″. *Herbert W. Hemphill, Jr.*

Top right: Horse and Rider Toy, New York or Pennsylvania,
circa 1850. Painted wood, height 17½″.
Mr. and Mrs. Harvey Kahn.

Right: Witch on Broomstick, New England (?), late 19th
century. Painted wood with twigs, height 12″.
Mr. and Mrs. Leo Rabkin.

83

Felipe B. Archuleta (b. 1910), though a New Mexican of
Spanish heritage, does not work in the *santero* tradition.
He generally carves large-scale animals like the bear
shown here, often based on illustrations in children's books
and natural history magazines. Tesuque, New Mexico,
circa 1973. Cottonwood, house paint, sawdust-glue
emulsion, and found materials, height 35⁷/₁₆".
*International Folk Art Foundation Collection in the
Museum of International Folk Art, a division of the
Museum of New Mexico, Santa Fe, New Mexico.*

Catalogue of the Exhibition

The catalogue has been arranged in chronological order. However, it should be borne in mind that at the present stage of scholarship in this field many of the dates are general or approximate.

Dimensions are in inches and are listed in order of height, width, and depth. Except where otherwise indicated, a single figure refers to height.

1 *illustrated p. 77*
Bacchus Tavern Sign
Norwich, Connecticut, second half of the 18th century
painted wood 26½ × 21 × 15½
The Connecticut Historical Society

2 *illustrated p. 76*
Grand Turk Tavern Sign
Boston, Massachusetts, 1789
painted wood 31 × 9½ × 7¼
The Connecticut Historical Society

3 *illustrated p. 48*
Red-Breasted Merganser Drake Decoy
Long Island, New York, 1790
T. Williams
painted wood with root head 4¾ × 16¼ × 5
Herbert W. Hemphill, Jr.

4 *illustrated p. 74*
Black Indian Whirligig
possibly 18th century
painted wood 10
Mr. and Mrs. Harvey Kahn

5
Female Figure
Sandwich, Massachusetts, possibly 18th century
chestnut wood with pewter eyes 16
The Marvill Collection

6 *illustrated p. 45*
Indian Rifleman Weather Vane
late 18th–early 19th century
iron 31
The Marvill Collection

7 *illustrated p. 46*
Hessian Soldier Whirligig
Pennsylvania, *circa* 1800
painted wood 36¾ × 12½ × 3⅝
Herbert W. Hemphill, Jr.

8   *illustrated p. 63*
Snake Trivet
circa 1800
iron 2 × 7 × 4
Mr. and Mrs. Harvey Kahn

9   *illustrated p. 57*
Face Jug
Montgomery County, Pennsylvania, *circa* 1805
stoneware harvest jug with salt glaze and blue cobalt
decoration 8 × 7 × 7
Private Collection

10   *illustrated p. 57*
Effigy Jug
Bath, South Carolina, *circa* 1817
glazed clay 7½ × 7½ × 7⅛
Augusta-Richmond County Museum

11   *illustrated p. 20*
Black Slave
probably New Orleans, Louisiana, 1800–1820
painted wood with human teeth and glass eyes 56
The Marvill Collection

12   *illustrated p. 48*
Flying Eagle
East Hampton, Massachusetts, 1800–1820
painted pine 36 × 42 × 42
Museum of Fine Arts, Boston,
John Wheelock Elliot Fund

13   *illustrated p. 75*
Schoolmaster Whirligig
circa 1825
painted wood 23½
Mr. and Mrs. Harvey Kahn

14a   *illustrated p. 6*
Hessian Soldier Whirligig
early 19th century
painted wood 26
Mr. and Mrs. Harvey Kahn

b   *illustrated p. 6*
Pair of Hessian Soldiers Whirligig
early 19th century
painted wood 27 × 13 × 4½
Mr. and Mrs. Robert Peak

15   *illustrated p. 51*
Doll
first quarter of the 19th century
wood 6
Private Collection

16   *illustrated p. 24*
Kneeling Sailor Ship Carving
Salem, Massachusetts, early 19th century
painted wood 27 × 29
Smithsonian Institution, National Museum of History
and Technology, Eleanor and Mabel Van Alstyne
American Folk Art Collection

17   *illustrated p. 63*
Serpentine Cane
Detroit, Michigan, early 19th century
grape vine 34½
Mr. and Mrs. James O. Keene

18   *illustrated p. 36*
"Protect Home Industries" Political Emblem
Charlestown Township, Pennsylvania, 1840 or 1844
William and Thomas Howard
painted iron and tin 118 × 55 × 6
Chester County Historical Society

19   *illustrated p. 25*
George Washington on his Charger, Jack
found in the vicinity of the Ohio-Pennsylvania border
near Pittsburgh, *circa* 1845
painted wood 13⅞ × 11 × 4⅛
Private Collection

20   *illustrated p. 18*
Peacock
New Hampshire, 1840's
painted wood 16 × 27
The Marvill Collection

21   *illustrated p. 26*
Medicine Man
probably Pennsylvania, *circa* 1850
painted pine with tin and taxidermist eyes 21⅞ × 5½ × 4½
Abby Aldrich Rockefeller Folk Art Collection

22   *illustrated p. 83*
Horse and Rider Toy
New York or Pennsylvania, *circa* 1850
painted wood 17½ × 18½
Mr. and Mrs. Harvey Kahn

23   *illustrated p. 51*
Man with Grapes
Wells, Maine, *circa* 1850
painted wood with ivory eyes 15½
Private Collection

24   *illustrated p. 17*
Centaur
Utica, New York, mid-19th century
Mr. Dines
painted wood 22½ × 22
Private Collection

25   *illustrated p. 18*
Standing Cockerel
Connecticut, 19th century
painted metal 24⅝ × 20⅛ × 6⅞
*Smithsonian Institution, National Museum of History
and Technology, Eleanor and Mabel Van Alstyne
American Folk Art Collection*

26   *illustrated p. 79*
Angel
Pennsylvania, 19th century
wood 8½
Private Collection

27   *illustrated p. 73*
George Washington
found in Cornwall, Pennsylvania, 19th century
painted wood 13⅞ × 4 × 4
Museum of Fine Arts, Boston, Gift of Maxim Karolik

28   *illustrated p. 69*
Death Cart
probably Servilleta, New Mexico, 19th century
cottonwood, gesso, and horsehair 44½ × 58½ × 23½
Taylor Museum, Colorado Springs Fine Arts Center

29   *illustrated p. 62*
Snake Swallowing a Frog
Georgia, 19th century
painted wood 31
Karen Sebiri

30   *illustrated p. 63*
Snake Cane
19th century
painted wood 35¼
Private Collection

31   *illustrated p. 45*
Cockerel Weather Vane
Ohio, second half of the 19th century
painted wood with metal straps 34 × 45 × 8½
Abby Aldrich Rockefeller Folk Art Collection

32
Horse and Rider with Large Pistol
possibly Pennsylvania, second half of the 19th century
wood, leather, and metal 16½ × 14 × 10¼
*Smithsonian Institution, National Museum of History
and Technology, Eleanor and Mabel Van Alstyne
American Folk Art Collection*

33   *illustrated p. 68*
Job
New Mexico, second half of the 19th century
gessoed and painted cottonwood and tin 14½ × 9 × 9½
Taylor Museum, Colorado Springs Fine Arts Center

34   *illustrated p. 45*
Curlew Weather Vane
Cape May, New Jersey, *circa* 1870
sheet iron with gold leaf 51 × 92
Mrs. Jacob M. Kaplan

35   *illustrated p. 9*
Policeman Whirligig
circa 1870
painted wood 8¾
Private Collection

36   *illustrated p. 26*
Seated Man with Derby
found in southern Ohio, *circa* 1870
wood 19 × 6 × 11½
George E. Schoellkopf Gallery

37   *illustrated p. 13*
Pair of Heron Decoys
probably Long Island or New Jersey, *circa* 1870
wood 32⅛ × 43½ and 40½ × 37
Memorial Art Gallery of the University of Rochester

38   *illustrated p. 38*
Indian Squaw and Scout
New Jersey (?), *circa* 1870
painted and stained wood
48½ × 16½ × 16 and 62 × 19 × 19
Herbert W. Hemphill, Jr.

39   *illustrated p. 72*
American Flag Gate
Hudson River Valley, New York, *circa* 1872
painted wood 46 × 56
Museum of American Folk Art

40   *illustrated p. 18*
Great Northern Loon Decoy
Penobscot Bay, Maine, *circa* 1875
painted wood 8½ × 26
Private Collection

41   *illustrated p. 13*
Horse with Fringe
found in Indiana, *circa* 1870-80
stained wood with silk fringe and
metal shoes 20½ × 20 × 5
Raymond Saroff

42   *illustrated p. 10*
Swimmer Weather Vane
New Hampshire, 1870's
painted wood, length 38
The Marvill Collection

43   *illustrated p. 79*
Dandy
1878
painted wood 14 × 1½ × 3
Timothy and Pamela Hill

44   *illustrated p. 11*
Nude Female Figure
New Hampshire, 1880's
wood 6
The Marvill Collection

45   *illustrated p. 54*
Two Black Figures
Hamilton, Ohio, *circa* 1880
wood and mixed media 56½ and 53¾
Collection of Michael and Julie Hall

46   *frontispiece*
Newsboy Trade Sign
Pawtucket, Rhode Island, 1889
painted wood and metal 42 × 36 × 15
Collection of Michael and Julie Hall

47   *illustrated p. 48*
Eagle with American Shield
Pennsylvania, *circa* 1870-90
Wilhelm Schimmel (1817-90)
painted pine 10¼ × 17¼ × 4¼
Mr. and Mrs. James O. Keene

48   *illustrated p. 78*
Knife Box
found in New York State, *circa* 1875-1900
painted wood 15
The New York State Historical Association

49   *illustrated p. 21*
Buffalo Bill
Pennsylvania or Ohio, 1880-90
painted wood 23¾ × 15½ × 6
Heritage Plantation

50   *illustrated p. 37*
Whirligig Weather Vane
southern Ohio, 1880-1900
wood 24 × 40¼ × 24
Collection of Michael and Julie Hall

51   *illustrated p. 81*
Reindeer Weather Vane
circa 1890
wood 21⅝ × 26⅛ × 13½
Lawrence Belles

52   *illustrated p. 66*
San Acacio
New Mexico, 1890's
painted wood 39 × 35 × 4
Mr. and Mrs. Jimmy Ernst

53   *illustrated p. 67*
San José
Mora County, New Mexico, *circa* 1890
José Benito Ortega (1858-1941)
gessoed and painted wood 49 × 16 × 10
Denver Art Museum

54   *illustrated p. 31*
Four Horsemen Whirligig
Ohio, late 19th century
painted wood and metal 15½ × 29 × 18
Herbert W. Hemphill, Jr.

55 *illustrated p. 83*
Witch on Broomstick
New England (?), late 19th century
painted wood with twigs 12 × 12¾ × 5¾
Mr. and Mrs. Leo Rabkin

56 *illustrated p. 75*
Baseball Player
late 19th century
painted and gilded wood 8¾ × 3¼ × 3
George Bird

57
Snake Cane
Indiana, late 19th century
inscribed: "IORM" (International Order of Red Men)
painted wood 36
Collection of Michael and Julie Hall

58
Animal Cane
Ohio, late 19th century
painted wood 36
Collection of Michael and Julie Hall

59
Alligator and Snake Cane
probably late 19th century
painted wood 41
Collection of Michael and Julie Hall

60 *illustrated p. 81*
Sow
Zoar, Ohio, *circa* 1900
painted wood 3¾ × 7
Private Collection

61 *illustrated p. 81*
Nanny Goat
Vermont, *circa* 1900
painted wood 6¾ × 6½
Private Collection

62 *illustrated p. 8*
White Head
circa 1900
painted wood 13¼ × 6 × 6¼
The Margaret Woodbury Strong Museum

63 *illustrated p. 9*
Railroad Conductor Whirligig
circa 1900
painted wood 15¼
Private Collection

64 *illustrated p. 23*
Horse (Blacksmith Shop Trade Sign)
circa 1900
wood with metal horseshoes 34¼ × 28½ × 3¼
The Barenholz Collection

65
Face Cane
circa 1900
wood 36
The Barenholz Collection

66 *illustrated p. 80*
Pair of Tigers
Portland, Maine, early 20th century
attributed to Augustus Wilson
painted wood 24 × 68 and 35½ × 79
Private Collection

67 *illustrated p. 53*
Preacher
found in North Carolina, early 20th century
painted wood 10 × 8½ × 3½
Mr. and Mrs. Roderick Moore

68 *illustrated p. 14*
Amish (?) Figure
Pennsylvania or Ohio, early 20th century
wood 28 × 8¾ × 6¾
Mr. and Mrs. Leo Rabkin

69 *illustrated p. 12*
Owl Decoy
New Jersey, early 20th century
painted wood with glass eyes and leather ears
14¼ × 5¼ × 5¼
Herbert W. Hemphill, Jr.

70 *illustrated p. 33*
Turtle Decoy
reportedly from South Carolina, probably early 20th century
painted wood 10 × 29 × 17
Collection of Michael and Julie Hall

89

71 *illustrated p. 81*
Hunter's Delight
possibly Vermont, 20th century
painted pine 19
Robert Bishop

72 *illustrated p. 82*
Touring Car
Long Island, New York, *circa* 1907
painted wood and metal 11¼ × 25 × 7¾
Herbert W. Hemphill, Jr.

73 *illustrated p. 25*
Bust of Abraham Lincoln
inscribed on base "C O" and "Feb. 5 [?] 1908"
painted wood 18 × 9 × 7
Mr. and Mrs. Bertram K. Little

74 *illustrated p. 50*
Buffalo Bill Cody
Vermont, *circa* 1910
cherry and maple wood with leather trim and ivory
buttons
18 × 14¾ × 9
The Margaret Woodbury Strong Museum

75 *illustrated p. 37*
Girl on a Pig
Killingworth, Connecticut, *circa* 1910
Clark Coe
painted wood with metal, horsehair, and ribbon
34¾ × 37 × 20½
Herbert W. Hemphill, Jr.

76 *back cover*
Miss Liberty
probably Connecticut, *circa* 1910
painted wood and sheet metal 82 × 23 × 31½
Collection of Michael and Julie Hall

77 *illustrated p. 47*
The Sport World Whirligig-Vane
near Gap, Pennsylvania, *circa* 1910
painted wood with iron, gesso, and composition shingles
56 × 90 × 14¼
Collection of Michael and Julie Hall

78 *illustrated p. 52*
Woman and Snake
South Carolina, *circa* 1920
wood 40
The Marvill Collection

79 *illustrated p. 23*
Figure in a Tin Cap
Michigan, *circa* 1920
painted wood and tin with marble eyes 43¾
Robert Bishop

80 *front cover*
Bicycle Boy Trade Sign
Brooklyn, New York, *circa* 1922
painted wood and metal 40 × 15¾ × 18
*The Brooklyn Museum, Dick S. Ramsay and
H. Randolph Lever Funds*

81 *illustrated p. 32*
Buckeye Family
Beaverhill, Tennessee, *circa* 1925
Joe Lee (d. 1941)
painted wood, tallest figure 56
The Barbara Johnson Collection

82 *illustrated p. 16*
Boy with Eagle
Balfour, North Carolina, *circa* 1929
Edgar Alexander McKillop (1878–1950)
walnut 51½ × 13 × 18
Greenfield Village and Henry Ford Museum

83 *illustrated p. 59*
Baron Samedi (Voodoo Figure)
New Orleans, *circa* 1930
painted wood and metal 32¾ × 13 × 6¾
Herbert W. Hemphill, Jr.

84 *illustrated p. 63*
Lizard
Woodbury, Tennessee, *circa* 1930
Fred Blair (*circa* 1901–1973)
painted wood 4¼ × 25 × 3½
Private Collection

85 *illustrated p. 27*
Woman with Tambourine
1935
Ed Davis
painted wood with metal and pearl earrings
17 × 5⅞ × 3⅜
Herbert W. Hemphill, Jr.

90

86　　　*illustrated p. 65*
Eve
Nashville, Tennessee, *circa* 1935
William Edmondson (*circa* 1865-1951)
limestone 32
Tennessee Botanical Gardens and Fine Arts Center,
Incorporated, Gift of Mrs. Alfred Starr

87　　　*illustrated p. 44*
Uncle Sam
North Reading, Massachusetts, *circa* 1935
painted pine 89¼ × 32¾ × 18
Museum of Fine Arts, Boston, Harriet Otis Cruft Fund

88　　　*illustrated p. 70*
Nuestra Señora de la Luz
Cordova, New Mexico, 1936
José Dolores Lopez (1868-1938)
cottonwood 40 × 18 × 6¾
Taylor Museum, Colorado Springs Fine Arts Center

89
Story of Job
Columbus, Ohio, 1938
Elijah Pierce (b. 1892)
painted wood 15 × 27⅞
Collection of Michael and Julie Hall

90　　　*illustrated p. 23*
Sturgeon Fish Decoy
Wisconsin, *circa* 1950
painted wood and tin, length 29
Robert Bishop

91　　　*illustrated p. 15*
Bull's Head
found in South Dakota, *circa* 1950
painted wood 19 × 20
Roger Brown

92　　　*illustrated p. 34*
Man with the Pony
Campton, Kentucky, *circa* 1950
Edgar Tolson (b. 1904)
painted wood 23¼ × 31½ × 11¾
Collection of Michael and Julie Hall

93　　　*illustrated p. 42*
Roadside Trade Sign
Waverly, Virginia, 1960-68
Miles B. Carpenter (b. 1889)
　a　　　*illustrated p. 42*
Watermelon
1960
painted wooden melon in metal handcart
melon 21½ × 39½ × 17; handcart 12¾ × 38 × 23
Abby Aldrich Rockefeller Folk Art Collection
　b
Two-headed Root Snakes
1968
painted wood 16 × 28
Jeffrey T. Camp
　c　　　*illustrated p. 43*
Root Monkey
1967
painted wood 30½ × 34 × 23
Jeffrey T. Camp
　d　　　*illustrated p. 43*
Pumpkin in a Wheelbarrow
1960
painted wood
pumpkin dia. 25; wheelbarrow length 72
Jeffrey T. Camp
　e　　　*illustrated p. 43*
Indian Warrior
1967
painted wood and fabric 67
Jeffrey T. Camp
　f
Standing Boy
painted wood and fabric 50 × 15 × 9
From the Contemporary Folk Collection of Jacqueline
and Ned Crouch
　g　　　*illustrated p. 43*
Root Bulldog
1968
painted wood 16 × 28 × 15
Lent by the Artist
　h
Watermelon Slice
painted wood 8¼ × 30¼
Mr. and Mrs. Roderick Moore
　j
Bull's Head
painted wood 21½
Herbert W. Hemphill, Jr.
　k
Indian Squaw
painted wood 54
Herbert W. Hemphill, Jr.

94
The Souls Beneath Defeats
Brooklyn, New York, 1969
Daniel Pressley (1918–71)
laminated pine 16 × 21
Marcia Wilson

95   *illustrated pp. 40-1*
The Fall of Man
Campton, Kentucky, 1969–70
Edgar Tolson (b. 1904)
painted wood
   a **Paradise** 12½
   b **Temptation** 15½
   c **Original Sin** 14½
   d **Expulsion** 12½
   e **Paradise Barred** 15½
   f **Birth of Cain** 8
   g **Cain Slays Abel** 13
   h **Cain Goes into the World** 14½
Collection of Michael and Julie Hall

96   *illustrated p. 84*
Bear
Tesuque, New Mexico, *circa* 1973
Felipe B. Archuleta (b. 1910)
cottonwood, house paint, sawdust-glue emulsion, and
found materials
35⁷⁄₁₆ × 62⅝ × 18⅛
*International Folk Art Foundation Collection in the
Museum of International Folk Art, a division of the
Museum of New Mexico, Santa Fe, New Mexico*

97   *illustrated p. 28*
Bathing Beauty
Nashville, Tennessee, 1973
Clarence Stringfield (b. 1903)
painted wood 57½ × 17¼ × 12
Estelle Friedman

98   *illustrated p. 29*
For Your Faith to Survive You Must Live It
Brooklyn, New York, 1974
Frank Mazur (b. 1910)
wood 56
Lent by the Artist

Selected Bibliography

Books and periodicals

"American Renaissance." *Creative Art,* November 1931.

Barber, Joel. *Wild Fowl Decoys.* New York: Windward House, 1934. Reprint. New York: Dover Publications, 1954.

Bishop, Robert. *American Folk Sculpture.* New York: E.P. Dutton & Co., 1974.

———. *The History of American Folk Sculpture.* New York: E.P. Dutton & Co., 1974.

Blasdel, Gregg N. "Grass-Roots Artist." *Art in America* 56, no. 5 (September–October 1968), pp. 24–41.

Boyd, E. *New Mexico Santos: How to Name Them.* Santa Fe: Museum of New Mexico Press, 1966.

———. *The New Mexico Santero.* Santa Fe: Museum of New Mexico Press, 1972.

———. *Popular Arts of Spanish New Mexico.* Santa Fe: Museum of New Mexico Press, 1974.

Brainard, Morgan B. *Tavern Signs.* Hartford, Connecticut: The Connecticut Historical Society, 1958.

Cahill, Holger. "Folk Art." *American Mercury,* September 1931.

Carlisle, Lilian Baker. *Eighteenth and Nineteenth Century American Art at Shelburne Museum.* Shelburne, Vermont: Shelburne Museum, 1961.

Chase, Judith Wragge. *Afro-American Art and Craft.* New York: Van Nostrand Reinhold Co., 1971.

Christensen, Erwin O. *Early American Wood Carving.* Cleveland: World Publishing Co., 1952. Reprint. New York: Dover Publications, 1972.

———. *The Index of American Design.* New York: Macmillan Co., 1959.

Davidson, Marshall. *The American Heritage History of Colonial Antiques.* New York: American Heritage Publishing Co., 1967.

———. *The American Heritage History of American Antiques from the Revolution to the Civil War.* New York: American Heritage Publishing Co., 1968.

———. *The American Heritage History of Antiques from the Civil War to World War I.* New York: American Heritage Publishing Co., 1969.

Dover, Cedric. *American Negro Art.* Greenwich, Connecticut: New York Graphic Society, 1960.

Drepperd, Carl W. *American Pioneer Arts and Artists.* Springfield, Massachusetts: Pond-Ekberg Co., 1942.

Earnest, Adele. *The Art of the Decoy: American Bird Carvings.* New York: Clarkson N. Potter, 1965.

Eaton, Allen H. *Handicrafts of the Southern Highlands.* New York: Russell Sage Foundation, 1937.

Fitzgerald, Ken. *Weathervanes and Whirligigs.* New York: Clarkson N. Potter, 1967.

Fried, Frederick. *Artists in Wood.* New York: Clarkson N. Potter, 1970.

Fine, Elsa Honig. *The Afro-American Artist.* New York: Holt, Rinehart and Winston, 1973.

Fuller, Edmund L. *The Sculpture of William Edmondson.* Pittsburg: University of Pittsburg Press, 1973.

Goldwater, Robert. *Primitivism in Modern Art.* Revised edition. New York: Vintage Books, 1967.

Gordon, Leah. "Vanes of the Wind." *Natural History* 81, no. 1 (January 1972), pp. 6–78.

Hemphill, Herbert W., Jr., and Weissman, Julia. *Twentieth-Century American Folk Art and Artists.* New York: E.P. Dutton & Co., 1974.

Hornung, Clarence P. *Treasury of American Design.* 2 vols. New York: Harry N. Abrams, 1972.

Horwitz, Elinor Lander. *Mountain People, Mountain Crafts.* Philadelphia: J.B. Lippincott, 1974.

——, and Moore, Roderick. *Contemporary American Folk Art.* Philadelphia: J. B. Lippincott, 1975.

Jahn, Janheinz. *Muntu: An Outline of the New African Culture.* New York: Grove Press Edition, 1961.

Janis, Sidney. *They Taught Themselves.* New York: Dial Press, 1942.

Kyerematen, A.A.Y. *Panoply of Ghana: Ornamental Art in Ghanaian Tradition and Culture.* New York: Praeger, 1964.

Laliberte, Norman, and Jones, Maureen. *Wooden Images.* New York: Reinhold Publishing Co., 1966.

Lipman, Jean. *American Folk Art in Wood, Metal, and Stone.* New York: Pantheon Books, 1948. Reprint. New York: Dover Publications, 1972.

——. *Provocative Parallels: Naive Early American/ International Sophisticates.* New York: E.P. Dutton & Co., 1975.

——, ed. *What Is American in American Art.* New York: McGraw-Hill Book Co., 1963.

——, and Winchester, Alice. *The Flowering of American Folk Art 1776-1876.* New York: Viking Press, 1974.

Little, Nina Fletcher. *The Abby Aldrich Rockefeller Folk Art Collection: A Descriptive Catalogue by Nina Fletcher Little.* Williamsburg, Virginia: Colonial Williamsburg, 1957; distributed by Little, Brown & Co., Boston.

Lord, Priscilla A., and Foley, Daniel J. *The Folk Arts and Crafts of New England.* Philadelphia: Chilton Book Co., 1965.

Mackey, William J., Jr. *American Bird Decoys.* New York: E.P. Dutton & Co., 1965.

Mills, George. *The People of the Saints.* Colorado Springs, Colorado: Taylor Museum, Colorado Springs Fine Arts Center, 1967.

Porter, James A. *Modern Negro Art.* New York: Dryden Press, 1943.

Shalkop, Robert L. *Wooden Saints, The Santos of New Mexico.* (Partial catalogue of the permanent collection of the Taylor Museum, Colorado Springs Fine Arts Center.) Feldafing: Buchheim Verlag, 1967.

Silberman, Charles E. *Crisis in Black and White.* New York: Vintage Book Edition, 1964.

Stoudt, John J. *Early Pennsylvania Arts and Crafts.* New York: A.S. Barnes & Co., 1964.

Stroessner, Robert. *Santos of the Southwest.* Denver, Colorado: Denver Art Museum, 1970.

Thompson, Robert Farris. "African Influence on the Art of the United States." In *Black Studies in the University* edited by A.L. Robinson, C.C. Forster and D.H. Olgilvie. New Haven, Connecticut: Yale University Press, 1969.

Exhibition catalogues

Akron, Ohio. Akron Art Institute. *Six Naives: An Exhibition of Living Contemporary Naive Artists*, 1973. Catalogue by Michael D. Hall and Herbert W. Hemphill, Jr.

Amherst, Massachusetts. Amherst College. *American Folk Art Exhibition*, 1974. Introduction by Frank Trapp.

Atlanta, Georgia. High Museum of Art. *Folk Art in America, A Living Tradition: Selections from the Abby Aldrich Rockefeller Folk Art Collection*, 1974.

Bloomfield Hills, Michigan. Cranbrook Academy of Art Gallery. *American Folk Sculpture, the Personal and the Eccentric*, 1971. Catalogue by Michael D. Hall.

Buffalo, New York. Albright-Knox Art Gallery. *American Folk Art from the Shelburne Museum in Vermont*, 1965. Introduction by Gordon M. Smith.

Chicago, Illinois. Renaissance Society at the University of Chicago. *Modern Primitives*, 1931. Essay by James Johnson Sweeney.

Chicago, Illinois. Renaissance Society at the University of Chicago. *Twentieth Century American Folk Art: The Herbert W. Hemphill, Jr. Collection*, 1975. Catalogue by Phyllis Kind.

Dearborn, Michigan. Greenfield Village and Henry Ford Museum. *Folk Art and the Street of Shops*, 1971. Foreword by Robert G. Wheeler.

Fort Worth, Texas. Amon Carter Museum of Western Art. *Santos: An Exhibition of the Religious Folk Art of New Mexico*, 1964. Essay by George Kubler.

Lincroft, New Jersey. Monmouth Museum. *Masterpieces of American Folk Art*, 1975. Catalogue by John Gordon.

Los Angeles, California. UCLA Art Galleries. *The Negro in American Art*, 1966. Essay: "One Hundred and Fifty Years of Afro-American Art" by James A. Porter.

Minneapolis, Minnesota. Walker Art Center. *Naives and Visionaries*, 1974. Introduction by Martin Friedman.

Newark, New Jersey. Newark Museum. *American Folk Sculpture, the Work of Eighteenth and Nineteenth Century Craftsmen*, 1931. Essay: "American Folk Sculpture" by Holger Cahill.

New York, New York. Museum of Early American Folk Art. *Catalogue of the Initial Loan Exhibition*, 1962.

New York, New York. Museum of Modern Art. *American Folk Art: The Art of the Common Man in America 1750-1900*, 1932. Catalogue by Holger Cahill.

New York, New York. Whitney Studio Club. *Early American Art*, 1924.

Rochester, New York. Memorial Art Gallery of the University of Rochester. *Signs and Symbols: American Folk Sculpture*, 1971. Catalogue by Isabel C. Herdle.

Sandwich, Massachusetts. Heritage Plantation. *The Herbert Waide Hemphill, Jr. Collection of Eighteenth, Nineteenth, and Twentieth Century American Folk Art*, 1974. Catalogue by H. R. Bradley Smith.

Tulsa, Oklahoma. Philbrook Art Center. *American Folk Art from the Ozarks to the Rockies*, 1975. Catalogue by Donald G. Humphrey.

Washington, District of Columbia. Smithsonian Institution. *American Folk Art: The Art and Spirit of a People, from the Eleanor and Mabel Van Alstyne Collection*, 1965. Text by Peter C. Welsh.

Williamsburg, Virginia. Abby Aldrich Rockefeller Folk Art Collection. *Wilhelm Schimmel and Aaron Mountz: Wood Carvers*, 1965. Text by Milton E. Flower.

Lenders to the Exhibition

Abby Aldrich Rockefeller Folk Art Collection, Williamsburg, Virginia; Museum of American Folk Art, New York, New York; Augusta-Richmond County Museum, Augusta, Georgia; Museum of Fine Arts, Boston, Massachusetts; The Brooklyn Museum, Brooklyn, New York; Chester County Historical Society, West Chester, Pennsylvania; The Connecticut Historical Society, Hartford, Connecticut; Denver Art Museum, Denver, Colorado; Greenfield Village and Henry Ford Museum, Dearborn, Michigan; Heritage Plantation, Sandwich, Massachusetts; International Folk Art Foundation Collection in the Museum of International Folk Art, a division of the Museum of New Mexico, Santa Fe, New Mexico; The New York State Historical Association, Cooperstown, New York; Memorial Art Gallery of the University of Rochester, Rochester, New York; Smithsonian Institution, National Museum of History and Technology, Washington, D.C.; The Margaret Woodbury Strong Museum, Rochester, New York; Taylor Museum, Colorado Springs Fine Arts Center, Colorado Springs, Colorado; Tennessee Botanical Gardens and Fine Arts Center, Incorporated, Cheekwood, Tennessee.

The Barenholz Collection, New Jersey; Lawrence Belles, New York; George Bird, Michigan; Robert Bishop, Michigan; Roger Brown, Illinois; Jeffrey T. Camp, Virginia; Miles B. Carpenter, Virginia; The Contemporary Folk Collection of Jacqueline and Ned Crouch, Tennessee; Mr. and Mrs. Jimmy Ernst, New York; Estelle E. Friedman, District of Columbia; Michael and Julie Hall, Michigan; Herbert W. Hemphill, Jr., New York; Timothy and Pamela Hill, Michigan; The Barbara Johnson Collection, New Jersey; Mr. and Mrs. Harvey Kahn, New Jersey; Mrs. Jacob M. Kaplan, New York; Mr. and Mrs. James O. Keene, Michigan; Mr. and Mrs. Bertram K. Little, Massachusetts; The Marvill Collection, New York; Frank Mazur, New York; Mr. and Mrs. J. Roderick Moore, Virginia; Mr. and Mrs. Robert Peak, Connecticut; Private Collections; Mr. and Mrs. Leo Rabkin, New York; Raymond Saroff, New York; George E. Schoellkopf Gallery, New York; Karen Sebiri, Connecticut; Marcia Wilson, New Jersey.

Photographs: Cat. nos. 3, 7, 18, 52, 69, 85, and 91 courtesy of E.P. Dutton & Co., Inc.; cat. nos. 14a and 14b courtesy of Kennedy Galleries, Inc.